Earth-friendly TOYS

The Earth-Friendly Series

Earth-Friendly Toys
How to Make Fabulous Toys and Games
from Reusable Objects

Earth-Friendly Fashions
How to Make Fabulous Clothes and Accessories
from Reusable Objects

How to Make Fabulous Toys and Games from Reusable Objects

George Pfiffner

John Wiley & Sons, Inc.

New York • Chichester • Brisbane • Toronto • Singapore

Library of Congress Cataloging-in-Publication Data

Pfiffner, George, 1923-
  Earth-friendly toys: how to make fabulous toys
  and games from reusable objects / George Pfiffner
      p.   cm.
  Includes index.
  ISBN 0-471-00822-2 (pbk.: alk. paper)
    1. Toy making—Juvenile literature.   2. Recycling
(Waste, etc.)—Juvenile literature.   [1. Toy making.
2. Handicraft.   3.   Recyling (Waste, etc.)]   I. Title.
TT174.P48 1994
745.592—dc20   93-45341

Printed in the United States of America
10 9 8 7 6 5 4 3 2

The publisher and the author have made every reason-
able effort to insure that the experiments and activities in
this book are safe when conducted as instructed but as-
sume no responsibility for any damage caused or
sustained while performing the experiments or activities
in the book. Parents, guardians, and/or teachers should
supervise young readers who undertake the experiments
and activities in this book.

Produced for John Wiley & Sons, Inc.,
by Tenth Avenue Editions, Inc.
Creative Director: Clive Giboire
Assistant Editor: Matthew Moore
Editorial Assistants: Diana Bryant,
Peter Wagner, and Dema Mantooth
Assistant Artist: James Immes

Foreword

Every day when we open our mail at the Environmental Action Coalition, we find letters from young people all over the country. We have probably received a letter from your town, maybe even from your school.

Sometimes the letters ask questions, such as "How can we start a recycling program?" or "How does a landfill work?"

Sometimes they report on recycling projects kids have started, such as "We use both sides of our notebook paper" and "Our Boy Scout troop collected 392,000 cans."

We are always glad to get letters like these because we have been working on recycling since 1970, when only a few people were involved. Today people are coming up with more and more ideas about recycling.

Young people have made a big difference. You have come up with new ideas. Many of you have started recycling programs in your schools. You have taught your parents and grandparents how important recycling is, so the whole family can help keep the environment clean.

This is a very important moment in the history of the environmental movement. Young people all over the world are working together to try to save our planet from being buried under garbage.

As you can see from the globe on the cover of this book, you are part of an international movement. We all have a lot to learn from each other.

Have you heard the slogan ***Reduce***, ***Reuse,*** and ***Recycle***? These three simple words will give you the key to taking environmental action.

Reduce the amount of garbage you create. This means telling the person in the store that you don't need a bag to carry what you bought.

Reuse means finding a new life for something instead of throwing it away. That's what this book is all about.

Recycle means taking used materials and making them into materials that can be used again. Like turning old newspaper into newspaper that can be printed on again.

Whether you are already an active recycler or are just getting started, this new series of books will give you many projects that you and your friends can make using things that would otherwise be thrown away.

If you enjoy the projects in this book, the next step is to show your friends how to make them.

You might also come up with some of your own ideas for projects. If you do, I'm sure the publisher would like to hear about them, so write them down. Who knows, maybe they'll be in the next book.

If you like the idea of recycling stuff, then you can look into what kind of recycling program your community has, or you can start a recycling program in your school. Ask your teacher for help.

But now it's time to get out your scissors and pencils and paste so you can get to work. Have a great time!

Steve Richardson
Executive Director,
Environmental Action Coalition

Contents

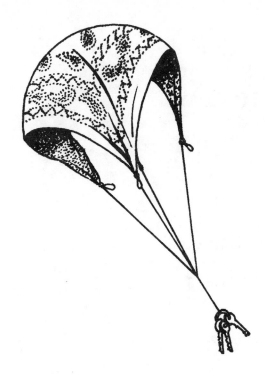

Foreword, 5

Being Earth-Friendly, 11

Getting Started, 12

THINGS THAT MOVE

Twirly-Thing, 21

Parachute, 23

Glider, 25

Flying Saucer, 27

Paper Pinwheel, 29

Spinning Top, 33

Funicular, 35

Skimmer, 39

Twirler, 41

Flying Fish, 43

Tugboat, 45

Locomotive, 49

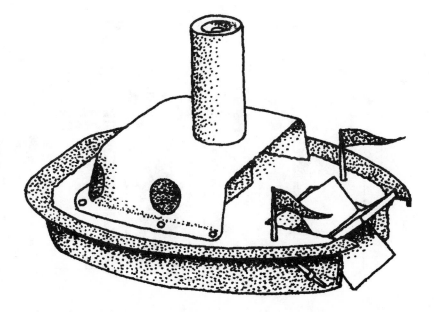

THINGS TO ENTERTAIN

Brown-Bag Mask, 59

Plastic Masks, 63

Newspaper Puppet, 69

Two Kazoos, 73

Bang-a-Can Can, 75

Juice-Can Stilts, 77

THINGS FOR FUN

Balancing Toy, 81

Tin-Can Telephone, 85

Construction Kit, 87

Nodosaurid, 89

Twister, 93

Cloth Doll, 97

Cradle, 103

The Castle, 107

GAMES TO PLAY

Picture Puzzle, 115

Ring-Toss, 119

Cap & Can Game, 123

3-D Tic-Tac-Toe, 125

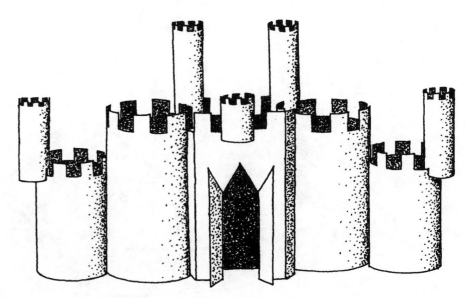

Being Earth-Friendly

Across the country and around the world, people are learning to reduce, reuse, and recycle. We have only one Earth, so we need to learn how to take care of it. We need to learn how to be "Earth-friendly."

Some people think that recycling is just about washing out cans and tying up newspapers. But we think that recycling is really about re-thinking—seeing the things around you in a new way.

When you start thinking about things in a new way, you can see that what used to be an empty tin can is now a telephone; what used to be an empty oatmeal carton is now the tower of a castle. This book, and the other books in this series, are about using your imagination to make new things out of old "trash."

There are 30 toys for you to make in this book. Every toy is made out of already-used materials. As you learn how to make cool toys, you will also be learning about how to help the environment. We've included information about recycling, and tips on how you can help.

But the most important thing about this book is that it's fun! Every project in this book is fun to do and the toys you make are fun to play with. Even when you've made all the toys in this book, the skills and ideas are yours forever—who knows where your imagination will lead you.

Getting Started

Your projects will be much easier if you follow all the instructions carefully. Here are some tips to get you started.

Before You Do Anything
Read all of the instructions and look at the drawings **before** you start making a project. The more you know about how the project is made, the easier it will be to follow the steps.

Level of Difficulty
Each project is rated according to how easy it is to complete. Here's a key to the symbols used to rate each project:

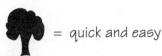 = quick and easy

 = little time and medium difficulty

 = time consuming and challenging

You might want to start with some of the easier and faster projects until you get the hang of following the instructions.

Work Time
Set aside plenty of time to work on each project, and give it your full attention. Your toys will turn out better if you don't hurry, and if you aren't distracted.

Work Place
After choosing a toy to make, decide on the best place to work. Some projects require more space than others. For example, the Glider can be made anywhere, because you're only folding paper. The 3-D Tic-Tac-Toe board needs a space where you can paint and leave your work to dry, maybe even overnight.

Materials
Get together everything you will need for the project **before** you start. Wash tin cans, bottles, and ice-cream cartons and leave them to dry before you use them. Put all the tools and materials on or near your work surface so that you can find them easily while you are working.

Some materials, such as scrap paper, empty cereal boxes, tin cans, and soda bottles, are easy to find at home. For some projects you will have to collect the materials you need. If you don't have enough oatmeal cartons to make the Castle, ask your friends or neighbors to save their cartons for you.

Don't be discouraged if you don't have exactly the materials we suggest. In many of the projects you can substitute materials. Ask your parents to help you decide if a substitute will work.

Symbols You Will Need to Know
❗ Steps marked with an ❗ need to be done with an **adult helper**. If you don't have an adult to help you, don't try this project.

✪ **Even Better:** Indicates ideas about how to make your toys more interesting.

Methods

The methods on the next few pages are shortcuts that are used in many of the projects. You may want to try them out before you start working on your first toy.

The Measuring and Marking Method will help you find the middle-point of a line, or help you cut centered holes.

The Pushpin Method will help you cut heavy material, like cardboard, and difficult shapes, like circles.

The Transfer Method will help you transfer patterns from this book onto cardboard, cloth, and Styrofoam.

The Center-Finding Method will help you find the center of any circle.

Once you get the hang of these methods, you won't need to read the instructions every time. But just in case, we remind you which pages the methods are on the first time we talk about them in each project.

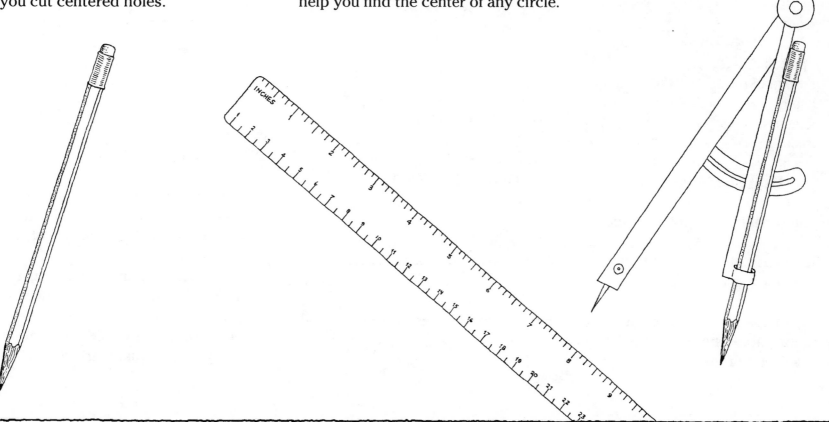

The Measuring and Marking Method

There are three kinds of measuring and marking that you will need to do in this book: 1. Finding the middle point of a line, (such as when you are tracing the pattern for the Doll, page 98). 2. Cutting a slot in something (such as when you are putting together the paddle wheel for the Tugboat, page 45). 3. Cutting out a "window" (such as when you make the frame for the Picture Puzzle, page 115).

You Need

- ☐ a pencil
- ☐ a piece of paper
- ☐ a ruler
- ☐ scissors

Instructions

1. To find the middle point on a line:

a. Cut a strip of paper that is at least as long as the line.

b. Lay the paper along the line, with one end of the paper lined up with one end of the line.

c. Make a mark on the paper at the other end of the line.

d. Cut off and discard any extra paper after your mark.

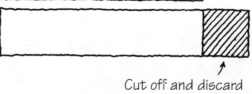

Cut off and discard the extra paper.

e. Fold the paper exactly in half.

f. Lay the folded paper along the line with one end of the paper lined up with one end of the line. The other end of the paper is the middle point of the line.

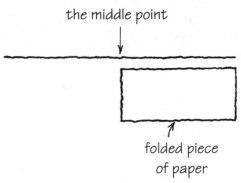

the middle point

folded piece of paper

2. To cut a centered slot:

a. Follow step **1** to find and mark the middle point of the edge on which you want to make a slot.

b. Use the ruler and pencil to mark the width of the slot on the edge. Remember that the middle of the slot should be the middle point that you have just marked.

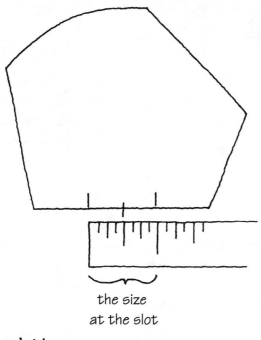

the size
at the slot

b. Use the ruler and pencil to connect the marks, as shown.

c. The lines you have just drawn make the outline of the window.

d. Use the Pushpin Method (see page 14) and scissors to cut out the window.

For example: If your slot is 1 × 1 inch (2.5 × 2.5 cm), place the ruler so that the $1/2$ inch (1.3 cm) mark is lined up with the middle point.

c. Once you have marked the two sides, you can easily measure, mark, and cut the height of the slot.

3. To cut a centered "window":

a. Follow step **2** to mark the dimensions of your window on all 4 sides of the piece you are cutting the window out of, as shown.

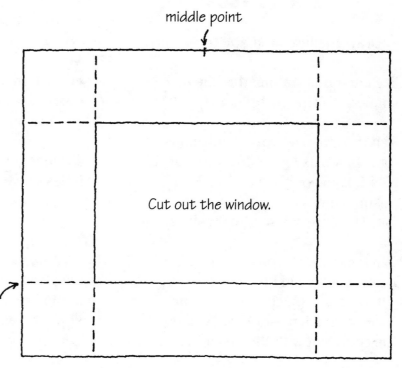

middle point

Cut out the window.

Draw lines to connect opposite slot marks.

The Pushpin Method

This method is useful when you need to cut heavy material or when you need to cut "windows."

Punch holes at even intervals around the shape you want to cut.

You Need

- ☐ a pencil
- ☐ a pushpin
- ☐ scissors

Instructions

1. Draw the line or shape to be cut.

2. Punch holes along the line or shape with the pushpin.

3. If the material you're cutting is **light** (such as light cardboard or thin plastic), you only need to make a few pushpin holes to start and guide the cut. Then use scissors to finish cutting.

4. If the material you're cutting is **heavy** and would be difficult to cut with scissors (such as heavy cardboard or thick plastic), you can make the entire cut with the pushpin alone.

a. Make pushpin holes at even intervals on the cut-line, as shown.

b. Now make holes between those holes.

c. Then make a third series of holes between the holes you've already punched.

d. Once you've punched a lot of holes close together, you should be able to pull the pieces apart or push the shape out.

5. If you need to cut a square or rectangle, first mark each corner with a pushpin hole. Then make your other pushpin holes working from corner to corner.

Then punch holes between those holes.

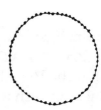

Then punch a third set of holes between **those** holes.

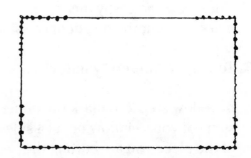

To cut right-angle corners, make pushpin holes along both edges.

The Transfer Method

For some of the projects in this book you will need to transfer patterns from the book to paper, cardboard, or cloth. This method will make that easy to do.

You Need

- ☐ a hard pencil
- ☐ a pencil sharpener
- ☐ a soft pencil
- ☐ tape
- ☐ tracing paper

Instructions

1. Working on a smooth, level surface, place the tracing paper over the design or pattern you want to transfer. Tape all four corners of the tracing paper to the pattern to keep the tracing paper from moving.

2. Trace the lines of the pattern onto the tracing paper using a soft pencil. Sharpen the pencil often so that the lines are clear and neat.

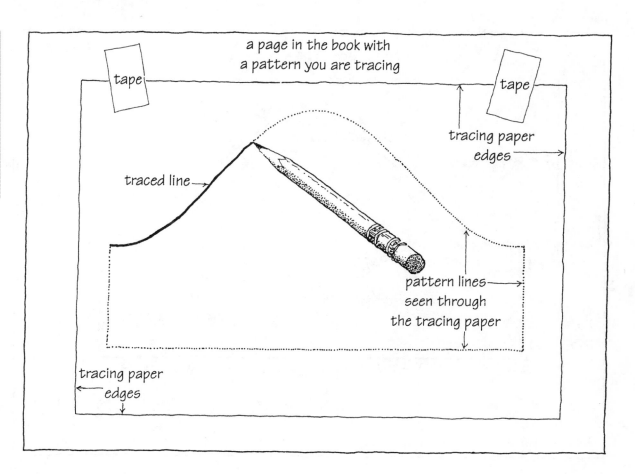

tape

a page in the book with a pattern you are tracing

tape

tracing paper edges

traced line

pattern lines seen through the tracing paper

tracing paper edges

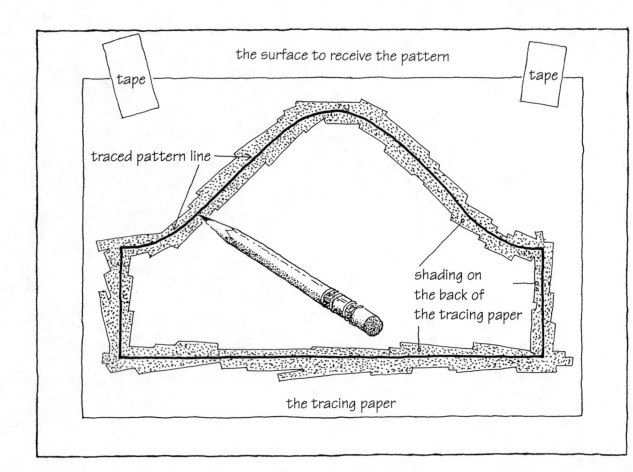

the surface to receive the pattern

tape

tape

traced pattern line

shading on
the back of
the tracing paper

the tracing paper

3. When you have finished tracing the pattern, remove the tape and turn the tracing paper over.

4. Use a soft pencil to cover all the lines on the back side with pencil shading. Use the side of the pencil lead to make the shading.

5. Turn the tracing back over and tape it onto the surface you've selected for the pattern. Transfer the pattern to that surface by retracing over the lines, this time with the hard pencil. Be sure to go over each line carefully.

6. You can lift up a corner of the tracing paper to check that the pattern is being transferred clearly. If it isn't, add more shading with the soft pencil.

7. When the entire pattern has been transferred, you may want to darken the lines with a pencil.

The Center-Finding Method

Use this method to find the exact center of any circle.

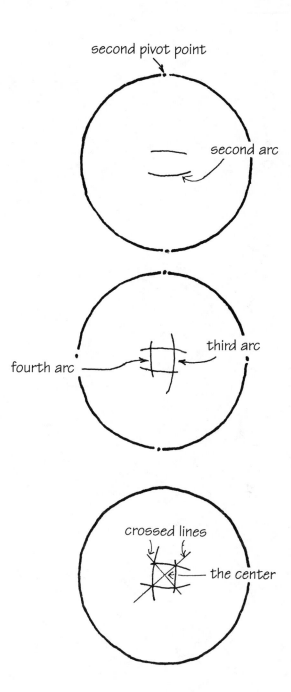

second pivot point

second arc

third arc

fourth arc

crossed lines

the center

You Need
☐ a compass (for drawing circles)
☐ a pencil
☐ a ruler

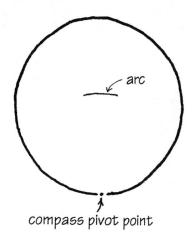

arc

compass pivot point

Instructions

1. Set your compass to a little more than half the diameter of the circle whose center you want to find. (The diameter is an imaginary line that goes through the center of a circle.)

2. Put the pivot (the pointed end) of the compass anywhere on the edge of the circle and draw a small arc (curved line) inside the circle.

3. Place the pivot of the compass on the circle directly across from the first point and draw a second small arc inside the circle.

4. Place the pivot on the circle one quarter of the way around from the second point and draw a third small arc inside the circle.

5. Now place the pivot on the circle directly across from the third point and draw a small arc inside the circle.

6. Use the ruler and pencil to draw two diagonal lines connecting the points where the four small arcs cross.

7. The point where the two diagonal lines cross is the exact center of the circle.

Things That Move

Twirly-Thing

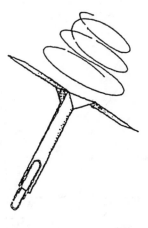

*The Twirly-Thing is a paper helicopter that you make
from an old magazine cover. Make Twirly-Things larger,
smaller, wider, or thinner. Make a fleet—throw them all at once.*

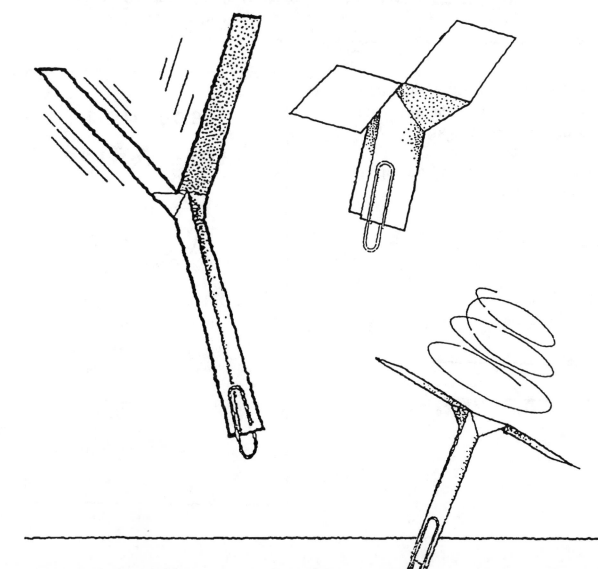

Instructions

1. Cut the paper to about 2 inches
(5 cm) wide and about 11 inches
(28 cm) long.

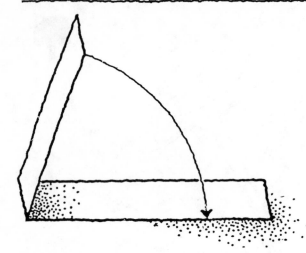

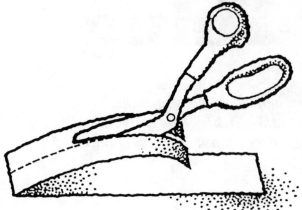

6. Slip a paper clip onto the bottom of the body over the ends of the flaps.

7. Holding the Twirly-Thing under the propellers, throw it into the air as high as you can. If it doesn't twirl, make certain the propellers point slightly up, or replace the paper clip with a larger one.

2. Fold the piece almost in half. The smaller part will be the propellers and the larger part will be the body.

3. Cut the smaller part in half the long way up to the fold.

4. To make the flaps, starting at the fold, cut at an angle almost one-third of the way into the body on both sides.

5. Fold the propellers and flaps as shown below.

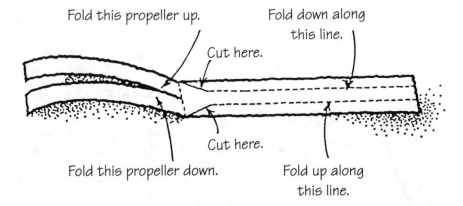

Fold this propeller up.

Fold down along this line.

Cut here.

Fold this propeller down.

Cut here.

Fold up along this line.

Parachute

This parachute gives a new use to old keys and an old bandana or other piece of fabric.

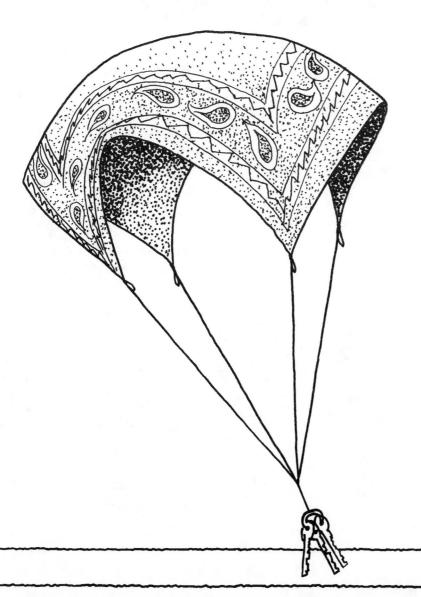

Instructions

1. Cut two pieces of string that are 24 inches (61 cm) long.

2. Thread both pieces of string through the key ring.

3. Tie the ends of the strings to the corners of the bandana. Use an overhand knot, as shown at right.

4. Hold the center of the bandana with the keys hanging down.

5. Loosely fold the sides of the bandana **in** and then roll the top **down** toward the keys, as shown below. Keep the strings from twisting when you roll them around the bandana.

Make the overhand knot like this.

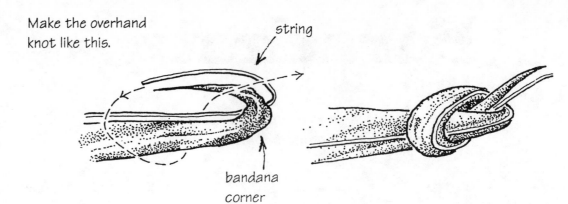

6. Stand in an open area outside that is away from trees, houses, and other places where your parachute could get stuck.

How to Fold and Roll Up
the Parachute

7. Throw the bundle into the air as high as you can. The parachute should burst open and settle gently to the ground. If the parachute falls too quickly or too slowly, adjust the weight by adding or removing keys.

✪ **Even Better:** Fine-tune the weight by adding metal washers to the ring instead of keys. You can also attach a small toy to the ring with a piece of string.

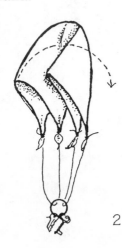

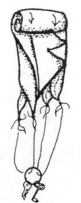
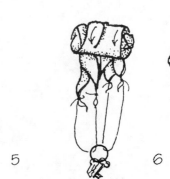
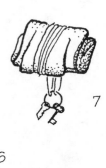

Glider

*You don't need to measure anything to make this glider.
It can be made out of any rectangle of paper, from an
old magazine cover to the front of a brown paper bag.*

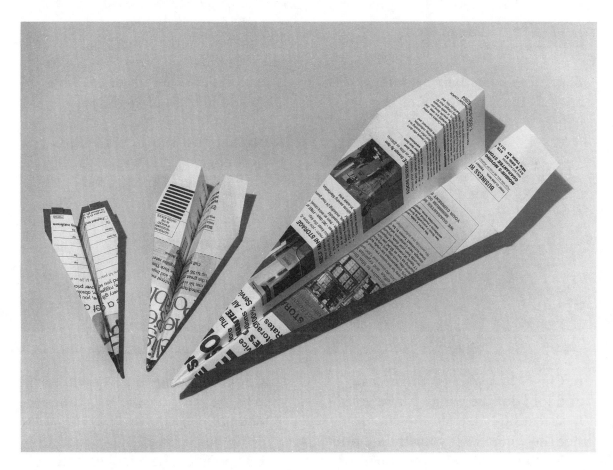

You Need

☐ a rectangle of slightly stiff paper

Tools

☐ scissors

Instructions

1. Fold the paper in half lengthwise. Crease the fold so it's easy to see.

2. Open the fold and turn the paper over.

3. Pick one short edge of the paper to be the front of your glider. Fold over both corners of the front edge, as shown on the next page.

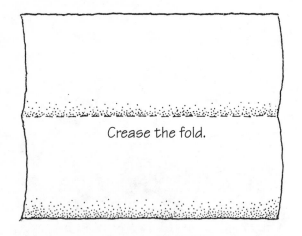

Crease the fold.

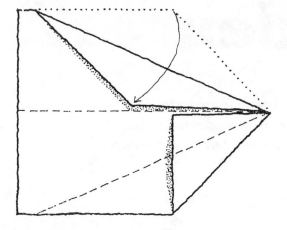

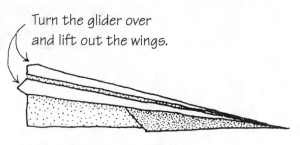

Turn the glider over and lift out the wings.

5. Fold again so that the outer, angled edges line up along the center crease.

7. If your glider takes a nosedive, you can make it fly better by making tabs in the wings:

a. Open both wings all the way up and hold them together.

b. Make two short cuts in the back edges of the wings about 1 inch (2.5 cm) apart, as shown.

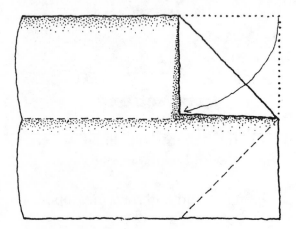

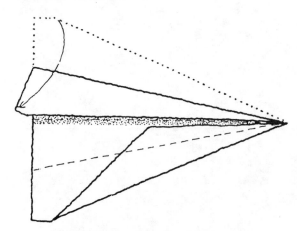

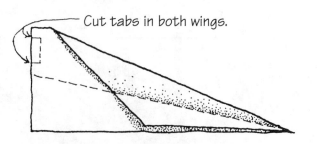

Cut tabs in both wings.

4. Fold over both of the new front edges so that they line up along the center crease.

6. Close the glider on the crease and fold out the wings. Make your first test flights. Hold the glider under the wings with your thumb and index finger. Pitch it point-forward into the air.

c. Fold the wings back down to flying position and fold the tabs up.

d. Experiment with folding both tabs down or one up and one down.

Flying Saucer

*When you aren't playing with this flying saucer,
it will look great hanging on the wall in your room. Best of
all, you can make it out of cleaned-up, old paper plates
and decorate it any way you want.*

You Need

☐ two identical, heavy paper dinner plates

Have on Hand

☐ newspaper
☐ white glue

Tools

☐ a compass (for drawing circles)
☐ a pushpin
☐ a ruler
☐ scissors

Instructions

1. Find and mark the exact center of one of the paper plates using the Center-Finding Method (see page 17).

2. Use the compass to draw a circle from the center with a radius of 3½ inches (8.9 cm).

3. Cut out the circle using the Pushpin Method (see page 14) and scissors.

4. Cover your work area with newspaper.

5. Place the cut-out plate on the uncut plate face-to-face. Notice where they touch.

6. Separate the plates and trail glue along the uncut plate's rim where the plates were touching.

7. Place the cut-out plate back on the uncut plate face-to-face. Make sure that the edges are lined up with each other all the way around. If the plates aren't exactly lined up, the Flying Saucer won't fly.

8. Once you are sure that the plates are lined up along their edges, set the Flying Saucer aside and wait at least 20 minutes for the glue to dry. Once the glue is set, your saucer is ready to fly. Just toss it in the air like a Frisbee™, with the open side down.

Recycling Facts & Tips

Did you know that:

- More than 73 million tons (66 million t) of paper are made each year.

- Paper is the single largest part of the waste we produce, making up nearly 40% of our trash.

- Recycling isn't only about reducing garbage, it's also about reducing pollution. For example, recycling one daily newspaper every day for a year can prevent nearly 14 pounds (6.3 kg) of air pollution.

How you can help:

- Most communities recycle newspaper. Is your family doing its part? We are already recycling nearly 1/3 of the paper we use, but every bit helps. Recycling one newspaper stack 4 feet (1.2 m) high will save one tree.

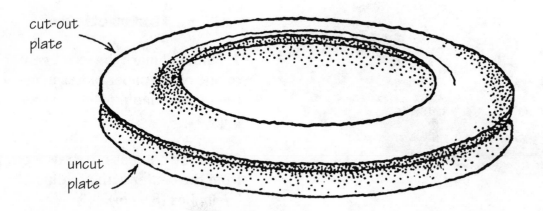

cut-out plate

uncut plate

Paper Pinwheel

Q: Why are pinwheels like recycling? A: Because both go 'round and 'round. Recyclable materials, like the magazines, boxes, and tubes used to make this toy, can have many lives.

You Need

- [ ] one 8-inch (20-cm) square of stiff paper (such as a magazine cover)
- [ ] five 1-inch (2.5-cm) squares of light cardboard (such as from a cereal box)
- [ ] one empty paper-towel tube
- [ ] one 4-inch (10-cm) square of heavy cardboard (such as from the back of a legal pad)
- [ ] one 6-inch (15-cm) bamboo shish-kebab skewer

Have on Hand

- [ ] white glue

Tools

- [ ] a compass (for drawing circles)
- [ ] a ruler
- [ ] scissors
- [ ] a sharp pencil
- [ ] a spring clothespin

Instructions

To Make the Pinwheels:

1. On the 8-inch (20-cm) square:

   a. Draw diagonal lines (from corner to corner) with a ruler and pencil.

   b. Make a pushpin hole at the center where the diagonal lines cross.

   c. Also draw horizontal and vertical lines through the center.

2. On one of the 1-inch (2.5-cm) squares of light cardboard:

   a. Draw diagonal lines.

   b. Glue the square to the center of the 8-inch (20-cm) square so

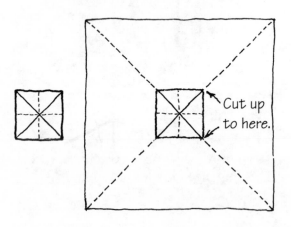

Cut up to here.

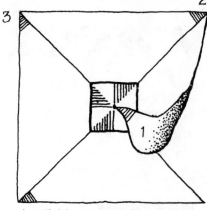

4   Fold points in like this.

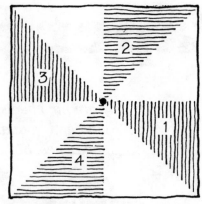

places to glue points #1 to #4 on center square (enlarged view)

that the diagonals of the two squares line up, as shown below.

   c. When the glue has dried, make a pushpin hole through the center of the two squares. Use a sharp pencil to enlarge the hole so that it will turn easily on the bamboo skewer.

3. Cut along the diagonal lines of the large square up to the edges of the small square.

4. Fold point #1 in toward the center of the large square and glue it to the small square, as shown above.

5. When the glue is dry on point #1, fold point #2 and glue it to the small

square. Use a spring clothespin to hold this point in place until the glue is dry.

6. Glue points #3 and #4 onto the small square, as shown. Use a clothespin to hold these points in place until the glue is dry.

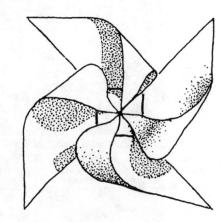

pinwheel with all points glued in place

To Make the Pinwheel Stand:

7. Glue the bottom of the paper-towel tube to the center of the 4-inch (10-cm) square of heavy cardboard.

8. Make a pushpin hole about ½ inch (1.3 cm) down from the top of the roll. Make a second hole directly across from, and level with, the first hole. Enlarge both holes with the point of a sharp pencil so the bamboo-skewer axle can turn easily in them.

To Hang the Pinwheel on Its Stand:

9. Draw diagonal lines on the four 1-inch (2.5-cm) squares and then make a pushpin hole in each one where the lines cross.

10. Push one of the squares—we'll call them "stops"—onto the axle at the pointed end. Push the stop down the axle until it is near the blunt end.

11. Place the axle, pointed end first, through the two holes in the pinwheel stand until the stop almost touches the stand.

12. Push a second stop onto the axle until it almost touches the stand.

13. Enlarge the holes in the remaining two stops so that they will turn easily on the axle.

14. Push one of those stops onto the axle until it is about 1½ inches (3.8 cm) from the stand.

15. Put the pinwheel on the axle and push the last stop on to hold it in place. Make sure that the stops on either side of the pinwheel are close to it, but not touching. Your Paper Pinwheel is ready to spin.

✪ **Even Better:** Drop pebbles, pennies, or old washers into the stand to keep your pinwheel from tipping over.

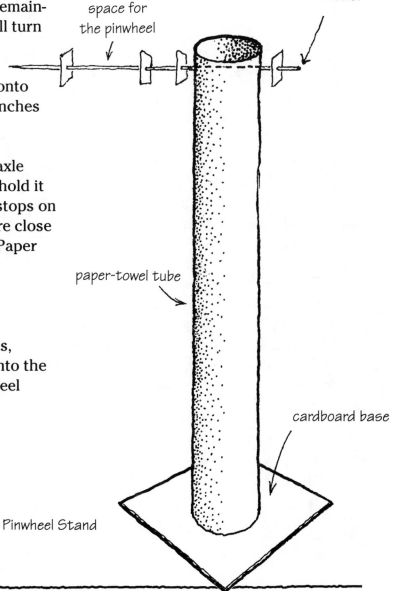

skewer

space for the pinwheel

paper-towel tube

cardboard base

Pinwheel Stand

Spinning Top

Make your own tops from cleaned-up paper plates and bowls. Go wild with the decorations.

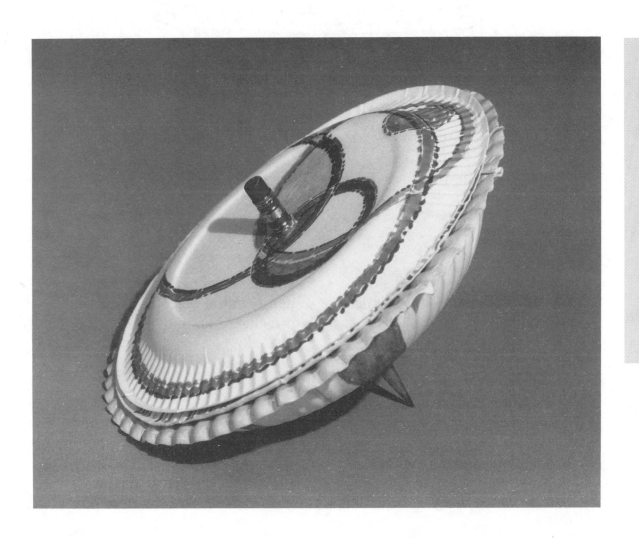

You Need

- ☐ three paper plates
- ☐ three paper bowls
- ☐ a sharp pencil

Have on Hand

- ☐ marking pens
- ☐ white glue

Tools

- ☐ a compass (for drawing circles)
- ☐ a few spring clothespins
- ☐ a pushpin

Instructions

1. Glue the paper plates together in one neat stack.

2. Glue the paper bowls together in another neat stack.

3. When the glue is dry (about 20 minutes), place the stacks of plates and bowls face down on your work surface. Use the Center-Finding Method (see page 17) to find and mark the center of each stack.

4. Make a hole through the center of each stack with the pushpin.

5. Enlarge the holes carefully with the tip of the pencil until they are just large enough to fit tightly around the pencil. Place the pencil point-down through the plates.

6. Trail glue along the edge of the bowls. Press the rim of the plates down onto the rim of the bowls so that they are face-to-face, with the edges lined up.

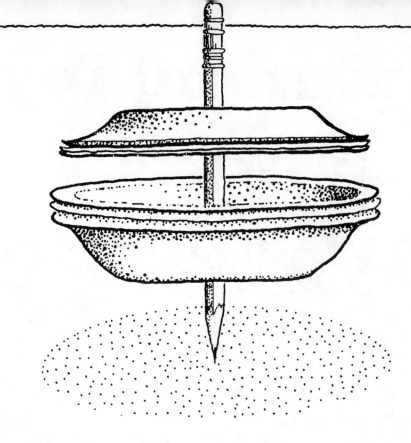

7. Push the pencil down through the hole in the bowls until the point sticks out the bottom, as shown.

   a. Make certain that the rim of the plates is resting on the rim of the bowls and that the pencil is straight up and down.

   b. Use clothespins to hold the rims together for about 20 minutes while the glue dries.

8. The pencil needs to fit very tightly in the hole. If it is loose, use glue to hold it.

9. When all the glue is dry, your top is ready to spin.

✪ **Even Better:** Paint your top with circular patterns. Spin your top on a piece of paper and see what designs the pencil makes.

Funicular

A funicular is a kind of cable car. It's used to get people up mountains and back down again. To make your miniature Funicular, you'll be reusing things like a plastic soda bottle and a table-tennis ball.

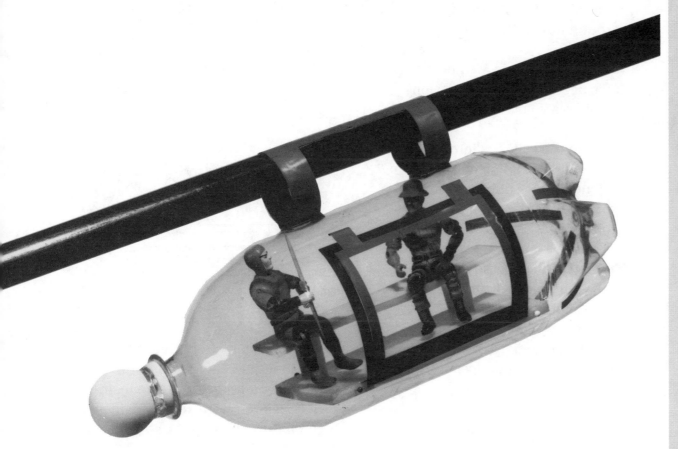

You Need

- ☐ one 2-liter clear, plastic soda bottle
- ☐ a sheet of light cardboard (such as from a cereal box)
- ☐ adhesive tape (colored tape would look even better)
- ☐ one toilet-paper tube
- ☐ one old table-tennis ball (it's OK if this is cracked)
- ☐ a long piece of smooth rope

Have on Hand

- ☐ masking tape
- ☐ a fine-point marking pen
- ☐ a ruler

Tools

- ☐ a compass (for drawing circles)
- ☐ a pushpin
- ☐ scissors

Instructions

1. Remove and set aside the soda-bottle cap. Remove any labels or stickers from the bottle.

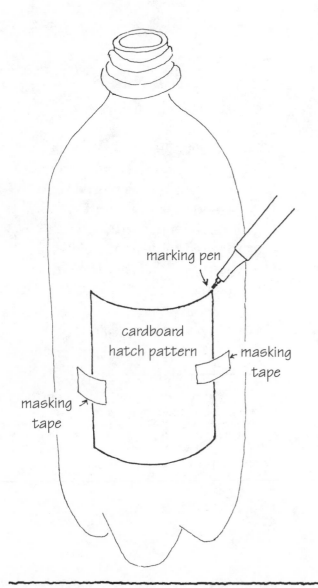

marking pen

cardboard hatch pattern

masking tape

masking tape

2. To make the hatch:

a. Cut a $2^1/_2 \times 4^1/_2$-inch (6.4×11.4-cm) rectangle of light cardboard as a guide.

b. Tape the guide against the middle of the bottle and draw around it with the marking pen.

c. Use the Pushpin Method (see page 14) to start cuts along the marks you've made.

d. Ease the scissors into the push-pin holes and finish cutting. You will need this cut-out piece for your hatch door, so make your cuts as neat as possible.

Note: If you ruin the hatch door, use your guide to cut a new one from another soda bottle.

e. Frame the edges of the hatch door and the hatch opening with colored tape.

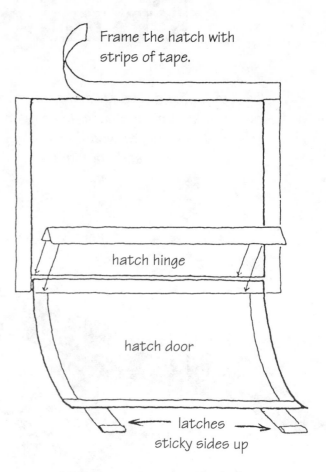

Frame the hatch with strips of tape.

hatch hinge

hatch door

latches
sticky sides up

f. Cut a piece of colored tape the length of the hatch door. To make a hinge, tape the inside of the hatch door to the inside of the hatch opening, as shown.

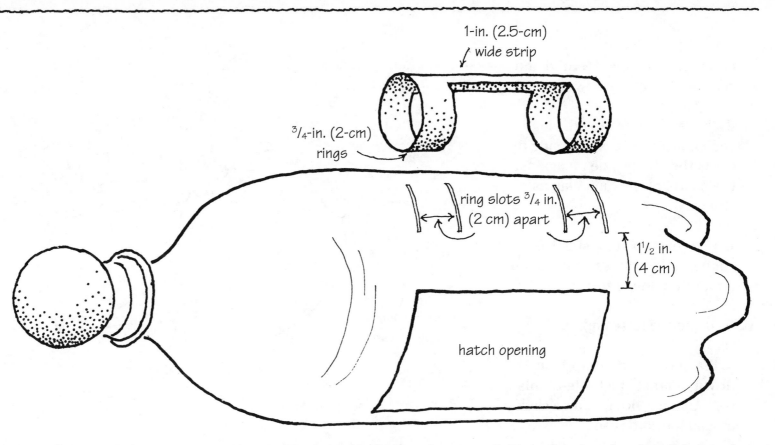

1-in. (2.5-cm) wide strip

$^3/_4$-in. (2-cm) rings

ring slots $^3/_4$ in. (2 cm) apart

$1^1/_2$ in. (4 cm)

hatch opening

g. Cut two small pieces of colored tape and fold one edge of each piece sticky side to sticky side. Stick these to the top of the door with part of their sticky sides facing in, as shown on the opposite page. You will use these "latches" to keep the hatch closed.

3. To make the slide bracket that will hold the funicular on the rope:

a. Use the Pushpin Method and scissors to cut the toilet-paper tube so that you end up with a $^3/_4$-inch (2-cm) ring at each end connected by a 1-inch (2.5-cm) wide strip.

b. Cover the inside of the connecting strip with tape to make it stronger and improve sliding.

4. To make slots for the slide bracket:

a. Place the slide bracket, connecting strip up, against the top of the funicular, about $1^1/_2$ inches (4 cm) above the hatch opening.

b. Make marks for the slots on the funicular on either side of the slide-bracket rings. Each slot is $^3/_4$ inch (2 cm) long and $^3/_4$ inch (2 cm) apart, as shown.

c. Use the Pushpin Method and scissors to cut the row of slots.

d. Pull a piece of tape through each pair of slots, sticky side up. Press the sticky side up against the inside of the funicular, as shown.

e. Use this tape to fasten the slide-bracket rings to the funicular. Cut off any leftover tape.

5. To make the nose cap:

a. Place the bottle cap **face down** against the table-tennis ball. Use a pencil to draw a circle around the bottle cap.

b. Use the Pushpin Method to cut out the circle.

c. Twist the table-tennis ball onto the mouth of the bottle.

Note: If the table-tennis ball is loose, use a little glue to hold it in place.

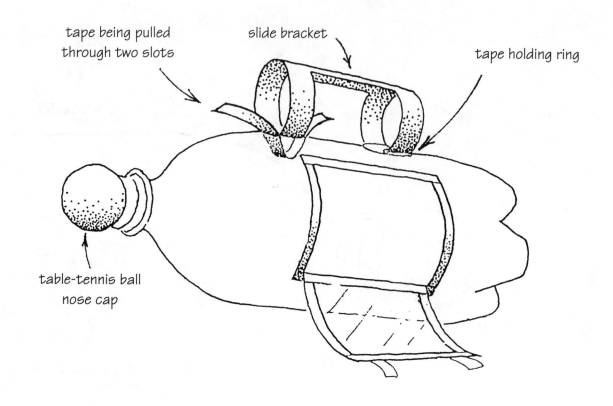

tape being pulled through two slots

slide bracket

tape holding ring

table-tennis ball nose cap

6. Put your rope through the slide-bracket rings. For the funicular to move on its own, one end of the rope must be higher than the other. Be sure to keep the rope taut. Your Funicular is ready to go.

✪ **Even Better:** You can also use the Funicular on a rope that is level. Tie long pieces of string to each of the slide brackets so that you can pull the Funicular in either direction. It's a great way to send and receive secret messages.

Skimmer

*Because of its large "wings," the Skimmer, made from
an old drinking straw and some magazine paper,
is almost lighter than air. You only need to give it
a little push and it will skim right along.*

You Need

- ☐ a drinking straw
- ☐ one 1 × 6-inch (2.5 × 15-cm) strip of magazine paper
- ☐ one 1 × 9-inch (2.5 × 23-cm) strip of magazine paper

Have on Hand

- ☐ scrap paper
- ☐ stick glue

Tools

- ☐ scissors

Instructions

1. To make the body:

a. Cut two 1-inch (2.5-cm) slits at each end of the straw. Be sure that these slits are parallel to each other on opposite sides of the straw.

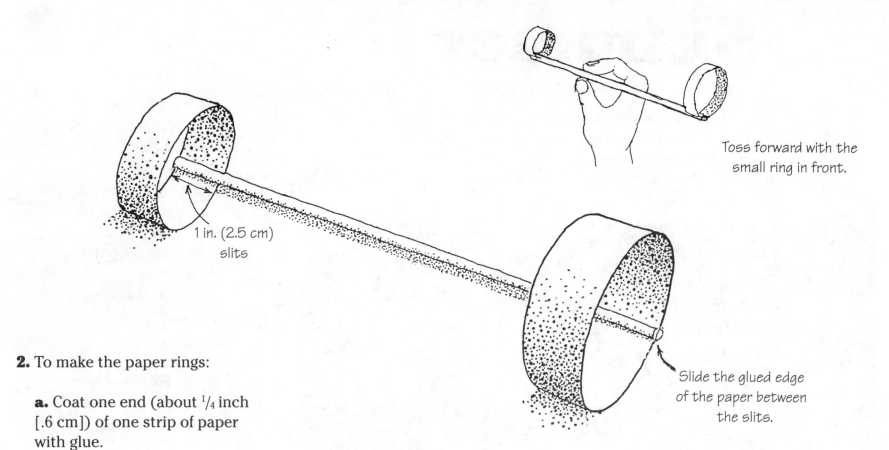

1 in. (2.5 cm) slits

Toss forward with the small ring in front.

Slide the glued edge of the paper between the slits.

2. To make the paper rings:

a. Coat one end (about ¹⁄₄ inch [.6 cm]) of one strip of paper with glue.

b. Turn the strip over and do the same on the other end.

c. Bend the glued ends together into a ring. Hold them together for a few seconds to allow the glue to dry.

d. Repeat steps **2a**, **b**, and **c** with the second strip of paper.

3. Slip one ring into the slits on each end of the straw. Make sure that the rings meet the straw at the points where they are glued together

4. Your Skimmer is ready to soar. Just throw it into the air, with the small ring forward, and watch it fly.

✪ **Even Better:** Try wider rings, such as 1¹⁄₂ inches (4 cm) or 2 inches (5 cm). If you want, you can decorate the paper rings with markers or colored pencils.

Twirler

A Twirler spins much faster and longer than a top. For the Twirler, you'll reuse a piece of cardboard and an old string.

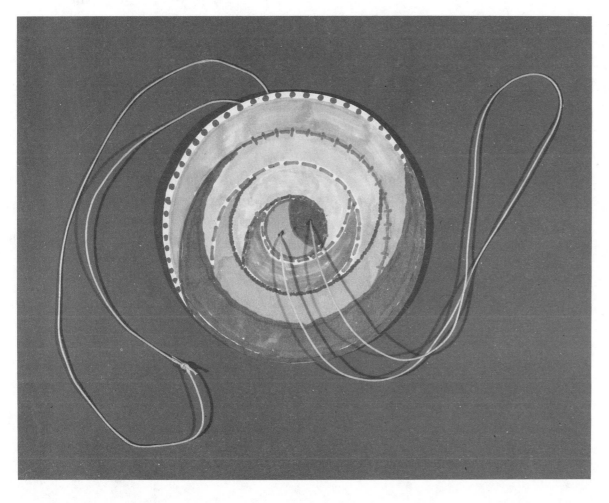

You Need

- [ ] one 5-inch (12.7-cm) square of light cardboard that is blank on both sides
- [ ] a piece of string that is 30 to 40 inches (76-100 cm) long

Have on Hand

- [ ] marking pens in lots of colors

Tools

- [ ] a compass (for drawing circles)
- [ ] a pencil
- [ ] a pushpin
- [ ] a ruler
- [ ] scissors

Instructions

1. Set your compass and draw a circle with a 2-inch (5-cm) radius on the cardboard. Use the scissors to cut out the circle.

2. Use the ruler and the pencil to draw a short line through the center mark left by the compass.

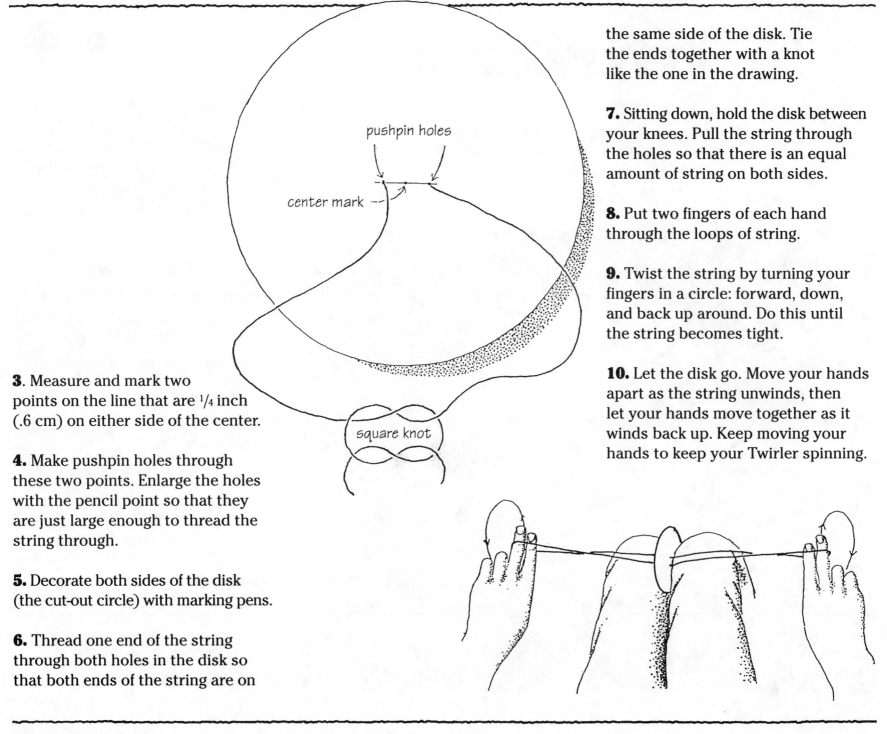

pushpin holes

center mark --

square knot

the same side of the disk. Tie the ends together with a knot like the one in the drawing.

7. Sitting down, hold the disk between your knees. Pull the string through the holes so that there is an equal amount of string on both sides.

8. Put two fingers of each hand through the loops of string.

9. Twist the string by turning your fingers in a circle: forward, down, and back up around. Do this until the string becomes tight.

10. Let the disk go. Move your hands apart as the string unwinds, then let your hands move together as it winds back up. Keep moving your hands to keep your Twirler spinning.

3. Measure and mark two points on the line that are ¼ inch (.6 cm) on either side of the center.

4. Make pushpin holes through these two points. Enlarge the holes with the pencil point so that they are just large enough to thread the string through.

5. Decorate both sides of the disk (the cut-out circle) with marking pens.

6. Thread one end of the string through both holes in the disk so that both ends of the string are on

Flying Fish

This fish would rather float through the air than swim through the sea. All your fish needs to fly is an old piece of magazine paper and your skill.

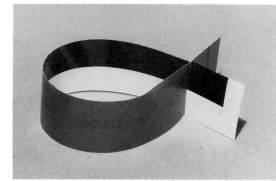

You Need

☐ one page from a magazine

Tools

☐ a pencil
☐ a ruler
☐ scissors

Instructions

1. Use the ruler and the pencil to mark a strip on the magazine page that is as long as the page and 1¼ inches (3.2 cm) wide.

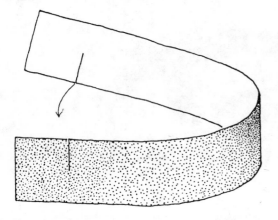

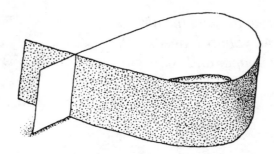

2. Use the scissors to cut out the strip.

3. Use the ruler and the pencil to mark two points on **opposite sides** of the strip that are 1¼ inches (3.2 cm) in from each end.

4. Cut a slit halfway into the strip at each point, as shown below.

5. Bend the paper into a loop, bringing the slits together. Push the slits together so that the loop closes, as shown above.

6. Hold one side of the paper loop between your thumb and first finger. Toss the Flying Fish into the air and it will gently flutter down.

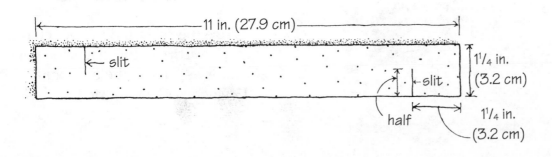

11 in. (27.9 cm)

slit

slit

half

1¼ in. (3.2 cm)

1¼ in. (3.2 cm)

Recycling Facts & Tips

Did you know that:

- Nearly 3 million tons (2.7 million t) of aluminum are thrown away each year.

- Nearly 2 million tons (1.8 million t) of that are containers like soda cans.

How you can help:

- It takes a lot of energy to turn raw materials into an aluminum can, but very little energy to turn an old can into a new one. The energy saved every time we recycle a can is enough to run a television for nearly 3 hours.

- Does your school recycle cans? If not, ask a teacher to help you start a program. A scrap metal company will probably pay for the cans you collect. Your school can use the money to expand the recycling program.

Tugboat

This tugboat is unsinkable and it moves under its own power. To get it moving, you'll need an old plastic dish, some Styrofoam, an egg carton, and a few other used items.

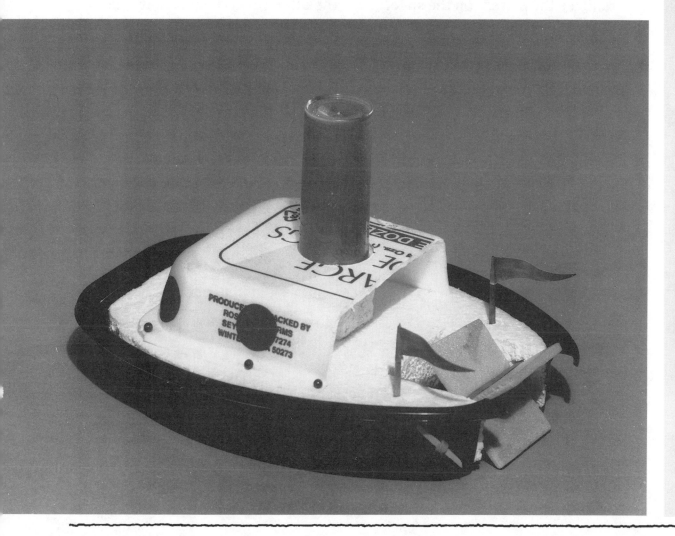

You Need

- [ ] one plastic dish from a frozen dinner that is about $5\frac{3}{4} \times 7\frac{1}{2}$ inches (14.6 × 19 cm)
- [ ] a sheet of Styrofoam packing material that is at least $6 \times 7 \times 1$ inch (15.2 × 17.8 × 2.5 cm), (such as from a stereo box)
- [ ] a piece of light cardboard (such as from a cereal box)
- [ ] one Styrofoam egg carton
- [ ] one plastic prescription pill bottle with its lid (Ask an **adult** for this. Be sure that the bottle has been washed out.)
- [ ] one rubber band
- [ ] one toothpick
- [ ] six pins with bead heads

Have on Hand

- [ ] Styrofoam glue

Tools

- [ ] a knitting needle
- [ ] a paper punch
- [ ] a pencil
- [ ] a pushpin
- [ ] a ruler
- [ ] scissors

Instructions

1. To cut a U-shaped place for the paddle wheel:

a. Mark a $2\frac{1}{4} \times 2\frac{1}{4}$-inch ($5.7 \times 5.7$-cm) shape with pushpin holes in the center of one end of the plastic dish, using the Measuring and Marking Method (see page 12).

b. Use the Pushpin Method (see page 14) and scissors to cut out the shape you have marked.

2. To make the paddle-wheel holes:

a. Make pushpin holes on either side of the U-shape you cut out in step **1**. The holes should be $\frac{3}{4}$ inch (2 cm) from the cut edge and $\frac{1}{2}$ inch (1.3 cm) from the bottom.

b. Enlarge the holes you've just made, using the paper punch. Be careful to center the punch over the pushpin holes.

3. To cut the Styrofoam deck:

a. Place the bottom of the plastic dish on the sheet of light cardboard.

b. Draw around the **bottom** of the dish with a pencil.

c. Cut out the outline with the scissors to make a pattern.

d. Place the pattern on the sheet of Styrofoam.

e. Cut through the Styrofoam by drawing around the edge of the cardboard pattern with a sharp pencil.

f. Press down firmly but not too hard. You will need to draw around the pattern several times before you cut all the way through. Don't worry if the edges are ragged.

4. Glue the Styrofoam into the plastic dish to make the boat deck.

5. Poke the knitting needle into one paddle-wheel hole, through the Styrofoam, and out through the other paddle-wheel hole. Pull the knitting needle out.

6. Push one end of the rubber band through both the holes with the point of the knitting needle.

7. Use short pieces of toothpick to keep the rubber band from pulling through the holes, as shown. If your rubber band is not taut enough to hold the toothpicks in place, try a shorter band.

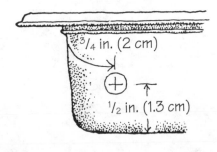

$\frac{3}{4}$ in. (2 cm)

$\frac{1}{2}$ in. (1.3 cm)

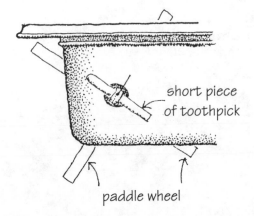

short piece of toothpick

paddle wheel

Put paddle-wheel pieces
together like this.

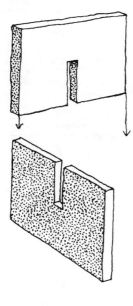

8. To make the paddle wheel:

a. Use the scissors to cut two
1 1/2 × 2-inch (4 × 5-cm) pieces
from the left-over egg-carton lid.

b. Use the Measuring and Marking
Method to mark a slot that is 1 inch
long × 1/8 inch wide (2.5 × .3 cm)
on the center of each piece.

c. Cut the slots out with the
scissors.

d. Put the two pieces together at
the slots to form an X, as shown.

e. Insert the paddle into the
rubber band you put on the boat
in step **6**. Make sure
that the two pieces
of the rubber band
are resting in
opposite sides
of the X,
as shown
here.

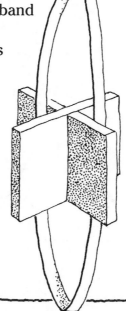

9. To make the cabin of the boat:

a. Cut off the egg-carton lid by
cutting along the hinge with the
scissors.

b. Draw a line across the top of
the lid that is 3 1/2 inches (8.9 cm)
from one short end.

c. Cut the lid in half along this
line and put the larger piece aside.
The smaller piece is the cabin.

d. Place the cabin upside down
on a piece of scrap cardboard.

10. To make the smokestack:

a. Turn the pill bottle (without its
cap) upside down on the inside of
the cabin.

b. Cut around the bottle with a
sharp pencil. The hole should be
centered side-to-side and a little
closer to the cut end of the cabin.

c. Put the cap back onto the pill
bottle. Trail a little Styrofoam glue
under the lip of the cap. Make

sure that there is glue all the way around the rim, where it sticks out from the bottle.

d. Turn the cabin over. Push the bottle up through the hole, so that the cap is glued to the under side of the cabin and the bottle sticks up through the top.

11. To attach the cabin to the deck:

a. Trail Styrofoam glue along the bottom edge of the cabin.

b. Put the cabin onto the deck and use several pins to hold it in place, as shown.

12. Your Tugboat is ready for duty. Set it in water, wind up the paddle, then let it go.

✪ **Even Better:** Add portholes by gluing on round pieces of colored paper. You can also make flags by gluing triangular pieces of colored paper to toothpicks.

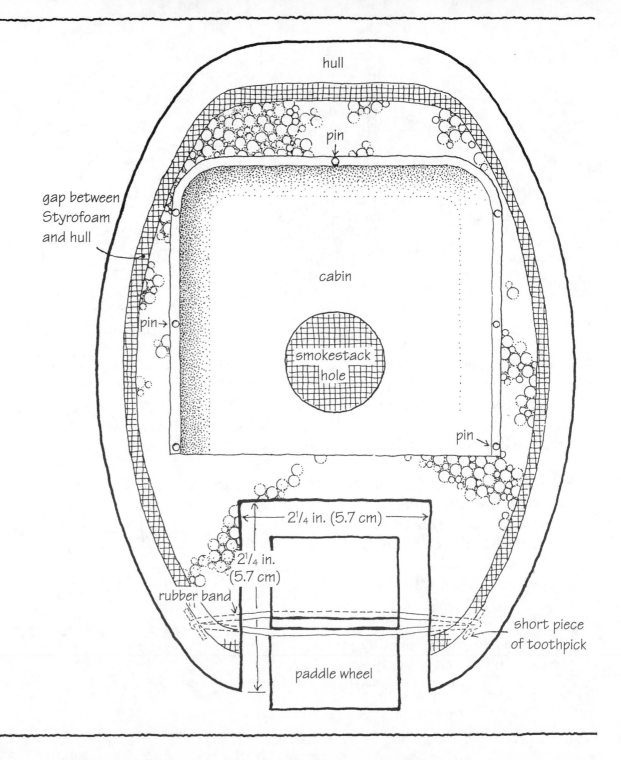

hull

pin

gap between Styrofoam and hull

cabin

pin →

smokestack hole

pin →

2¼ in. (5.7 cm)

2¼ in. (5.7 cm)

rubber band

short piece of toothpick

paddle wheel

Locomotive

The locomotive is the biggest project in this book. Before you start, you will need a lot of used items, such as peanut containers and an oatmeal carton, empty and clean.

You Need

- [ ] one facial-tissue box, $10 \times 4\frac{1}{2} \times$ 3 inches ($25.4 \times 11.4 \times 7.6$ cm)
- [ ] two 12-ounce (355-ml) peanut containers with plastic lids (these must be the kind of containers that have metal bottoms and cardboard sides)
- [ ] two $6\frac{1}{2}$-ounce (200-ml) peanut containers with plastic lids
- [ ] two plastic and metal lids from 8-ounce (235-ml) peanut jars
- [ ] three 6-inch (15.2-cm) bamboo shish-kebab skewers
- [ ] two soft pink-rubber erasers
- [ ] one 18-ounce (510-g) round oatmeal carton
- [ ] two $\frac{1}{2}$-gallon (2-liter) milk or juice cartons

(continued on the next page)

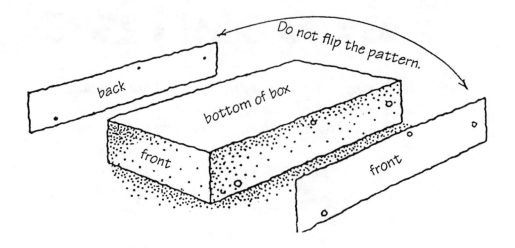

back

bottom of box

Do not flip the pattern.

front

front

You need (continued)

- ☐ three plastic prescription pill bottles (Ask an **adult** for these. Be sure they are washed out before you use them.) Two should be about 1 inch (2.5 cm) in diameter and one about 1¼ inches (3.2 cm) in diameter.
- ☐ one plastic lid from a prescription pill bottle
- ☐ a cotton ball

Have on Hand

- ☐ masking tape
- ☐ a pencil
- ☐ scrap cardboard
- ☐ three large paper clips
- ☐ white glue

Tools

- ❗ an awl
- ☐ a butter knife
- ☐ a compass (for drawing circles)
- ❗ a matte knife
- ☐ a pushpin
- ☐ a ruler
- ☐ scissors

Instructions

1. To make the locomotive platform:

a. Use the ruler and pencil to draw two points 1¼ inches (3 cm) up from the bottom of the tissue box on all four sides.

b. Draw a line connecting the points on each side.

c. Use the Pushpin Method (see page 14) to cut along these lines. If the flaps of the box come loose, glue them down.

d. Trace the Axle Holes Pattern (page 56) onto a piece of paper and cut it out. Use the pattern to mark matching pairs of holes on both sides of the tissue-box platform, as shown above.

e. Carefully poke through the holes with a pushpin. The holes on one side of the platform must line up exactly with the holes on the other side.

f. Enlarge the holes with the point of a pencil so that the bamboo-skewer axles will fit.

2. To make the wheels:

a. To mark the four peanut containers ¹/₂ to ³/₄ inch (1.3-2 cm) from the bottom, use the following method: Working on a flat surface, put a pencil down on one of the erasers. Hold the pencil firmly and turn the container around against the pencil point to mark a circle around the container, as shown below.

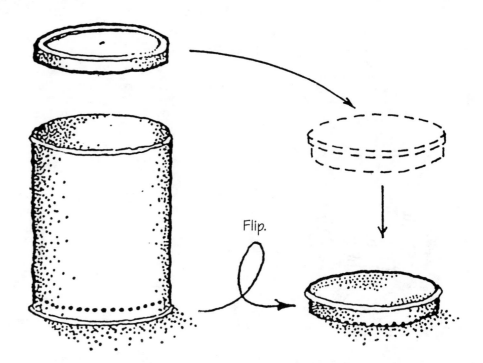

Flip.

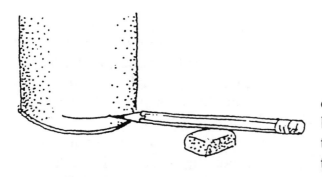

b. Use the Pushpin Method and the butter knife to cut off the bottoms of the cans.

c. Slip the four yellow, plastic peanut-container lids over the metal container bottoms. These will be the four back wheels.

d. The center point of the lid is a bump you can see on the inside of the lid. Punch a hole right through the bump with a pushpin.

Neat trick: Place an eraser under the center point as a support and to prevent damage to your work surface.

e. Remove the plastic lids and slip them onto the other side of the bottoms, as shown on the next page.

!f. Have an **adult helper** use the awl to enlarge the holes through the centers of the wheels so that they will spin on the bamboo-skewer axles. Also have your **adult helper** punch holes in the two smaller plastic and metal lids.

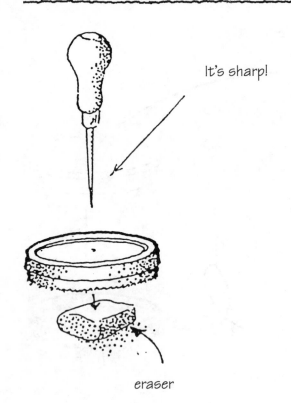

It's sharp!

eraser

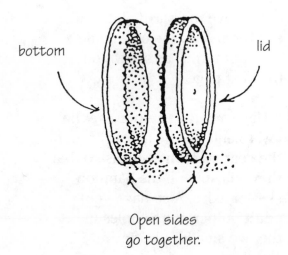

bottom

lid

Open sides
go together.

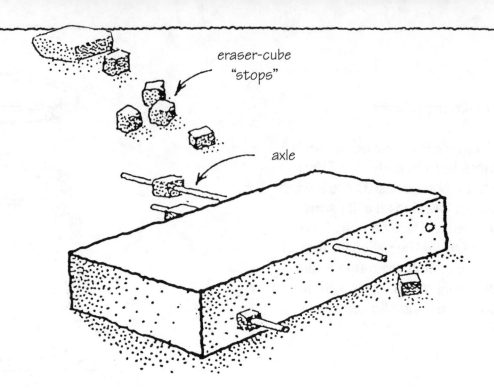

eraser-cube
"stops"

axle

3. To make the wheel stops:

! a. Have an **adult helper** cut
12 cubes from the rubber erasers
with a matte knife. We'll call these
cubes "stops."

b. Make a hole through the center
of each stop with the pushpin.
Have an **adult helper** enlarge the
holes with the awl so that the
bamboo-skewer axles will just
fit through them.

c. Push one stop onto each
bamboo-skewer axle and insert
each axle through the matching
pairs of holes in the platform.

d. Push a second stop onto the
other end of each axle. Center
the axles on the platform with
the stops just touching the sides.

e. Place the front pair of (smaller)
wheels on the axles, and put stops
outside to hold the wheels in place.
Now do the same with the four
large back wheels.

4. To make the cowcatcher:

a. Trace the Cowcatcher Pattern (page 56) onto a piece of paper and cut it out. Use the pattern to mark the cowcatcher on the first juice carton, as shown below.

b. Use the Pushpin Method and scissors to cut out the cowcatcher.

c. Crease along the dotted line, as shown in the diagram. Fold the flaps under and glue them to the front of the platform. Hold the cowcatcher in place with paper clips until the glue is dry.

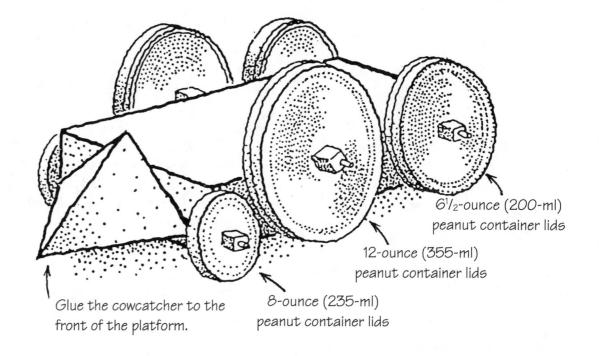

6½-ounce (200-ml) peanut container lids

12-ounce (355-ml) peanut container lids

8-ounce (235-ml) peanut container lids

Glue the cowcatcher to the front of the platform.

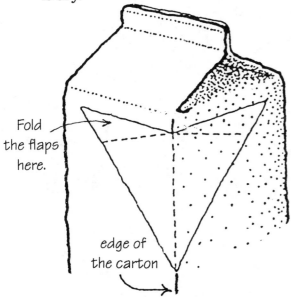

Fold the flaps here.

edge of the carton

5. To make the boiler:

a. Place one of the prescription pill bottles against the side of the oatmeal carton, along the edge of the label, about one third of the way from the bottom. Use the pencil to trace around the bottom of the bottle. Do the same with the other two bottles, making the marks all in a row. These will be the smokestack holes.

b. Cut out the circles using the Pushpin Method and scissors. Make the pushpin holes along the inside of the circles so the smokestacks will fit snugly.

Bracket Pattern

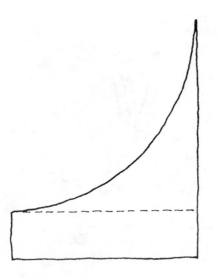

b. Use scissors to cut out the four brackets.

c. Fold the bracket tabs, as shown below.

d. Glue the brackets to the top of the locomotive platform, as shown below. Wait at least 20 minutes for the glue to dry before going on to the next step.

e. Trail glue along the curved edges of the brackets and place the boiler on them so that the smokestack holes point straight up and the larger hole is at the back. The front of the boiler should touch the back of the cowcatcher.

f. Push the pill bottles into the smokestack holes, as shown in the photo at the beginning of this project.

6. To make the four boiler brackets:

a. Trace the Bracket Pattern (above) onto a piece of paper. Then use the Transfer Method (see page 15) to copy it onto scrap cardboard four times.

Note: It will be easier to cut out the brackets if you position them at the edges of the cardboard.

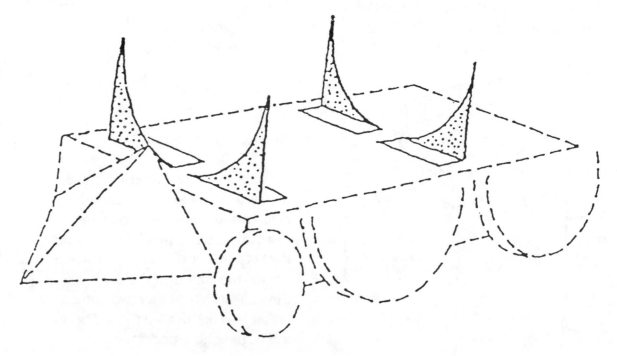

7. To make the cab, as shown in the diagram below:

a. Glue the spout of the second juice carton closed. Use a paper clip to hold it in place until the glue is dry.

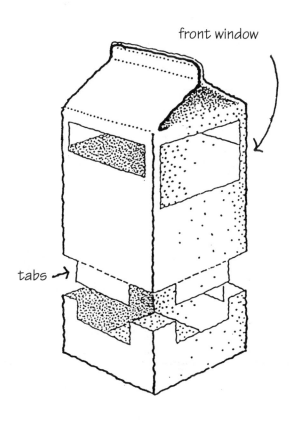

front window

tabs →

b. Mark three tabs on the carton about 2 inches (5 cm) from the bottom, measuring $1/2 \times 2$ inches (1.3×5 cm). No tab is needed for the back of the cab.

c. Use the Pushpin Method to cut out the tabs and to cut straight across the back.

d. Use the Pushpin Method and scissors to cut one window out of each side of the carton. The front window should be slightly larger than the other windows.

e. To attach the cab to the platform, fold the tabs in, and glue them to the platform right behind the boiler. The large window faces front. The back of the cab will hang off the end of the platform by about 1 inch (2.5 cm).

8. The finishing touches: Apply glue to the top of the largest smokestack and put a smokelike puff of absorbent cotton on the glue. Glue a pill-bottle cap on the front of the boiler for a headlight, and your locomotive is ready to roll.

Recycling Facts & Tips

Did you know that:

- Nearly 35% of the trees cut every year become paper.

- If we recycled half the paper we use each year, we would cut 20 million fewer acres of forest.

- Packaging makes up nearly one-third of our trash each year.

How you can help:

- Try to buy less packaging. For example, do you need a bag for everything you buy? Use your backpack or tote bag instead.

- Some foods—like rice, beans, pasta, cereal, and even candy—are available "in bulk." That means that you can buy them in a plain bag, without extra boxes, bags, jars, or plastic.

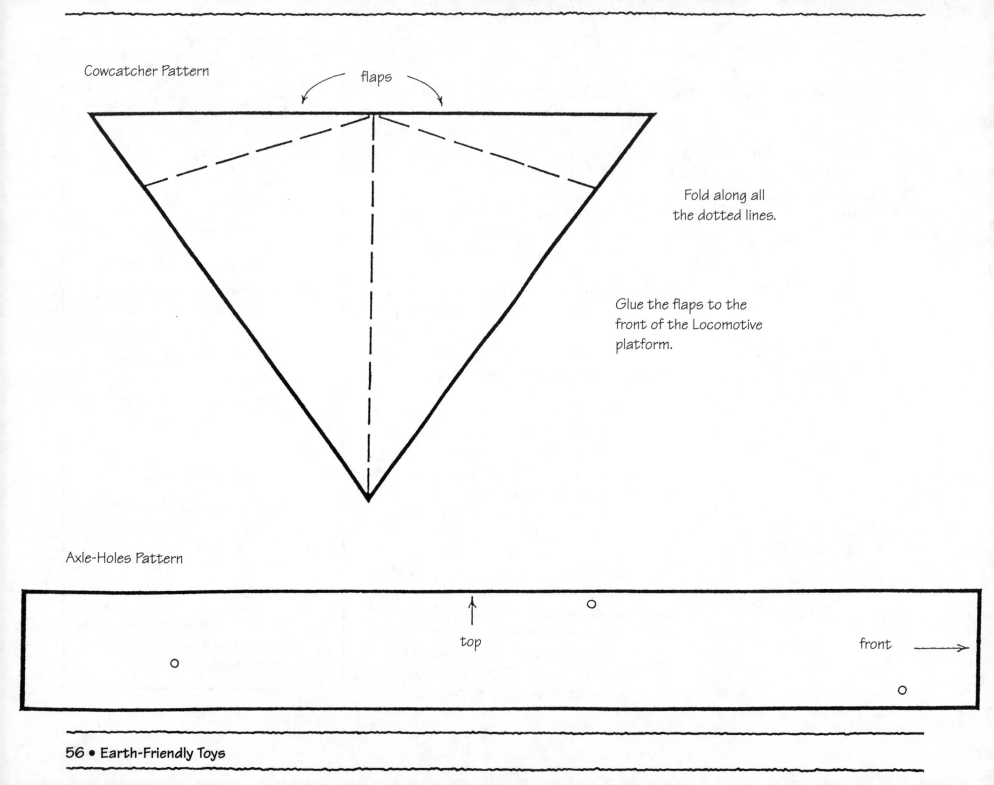

Cowcatcher Pattern

flaps

Fold along all
the dotted lines.

Glue the flaps to the
front of the Locomotive
platform.

Axle-Holes Pattern

top

front

Things to
Entertain

Brown-Bag Mask

*Cut, bend, and glue a brown-paper bag and you've got a mask.
You can leave it brown or decorate it any way you like.*

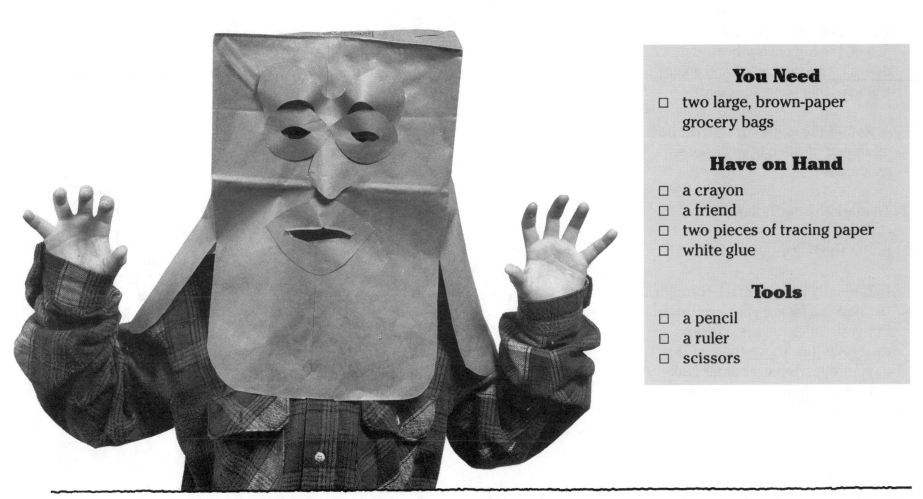

You Need

- ☐ two large, brown-paper grocery bags

Have on Hand

- ☐ a crayon
- ☐ a friend
- ☐ two pieces of tracing paper
- ☐ white glue

Tools

- ☐ a pencil
- ☐ a ruler
- ☐ scissors

Instructions

1. Open up one of the bags and turn it so that the open end faces you.

a. Cut in about 7 inches (18 cm) along each creased edge.

b. Put the bag over your head. The bottom of the bag should rest just on the top of your head. If it doesn't, take the bag off and cut in a little farther along the edges.

c. Round the eight corners of the open end of the bag with scissors, as shown.

2. To mark the eye holes:

a. Put the bag on your head.

b. Carefully feel your face through the bag and locate your eyebrows. Put your index fingers on your eyebrows just above the middles of your eyes. Have a helper carefully mark around your fingers.

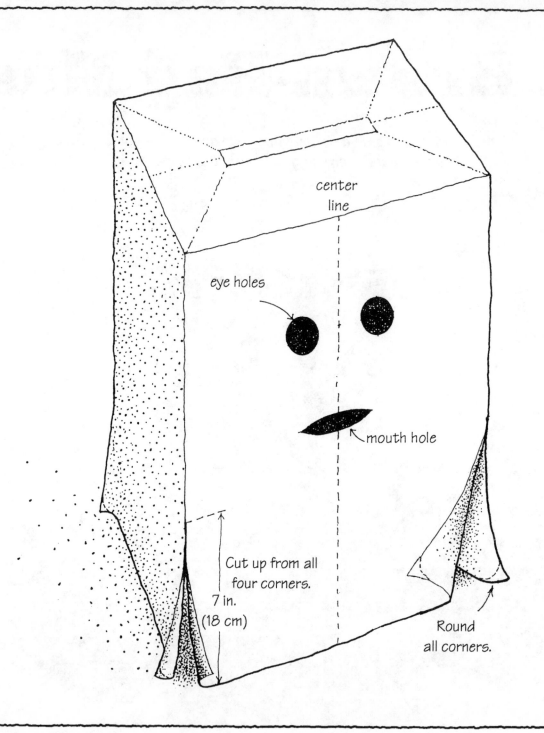

center line

eye holes

mouth hole

Cut up from all four corners.

7 in. (18 cm)

Round all corners.

c. Take the bag off your head.

d. Make crayon marks 1 inch (2.5 cm) straight below the marks your helper made.

e. Cut small circles out around the second crayon marks you made.

f. Try the mask on. If you can't see out well, make the holes a little larger.

3. To mark the mouth hole:

a. Put the bag on your head.

b. Carefully feel your face through the mask and locate your mouth. Use a crayon to draw an outline around your mouth.

c. Take the bag off your head.

d. Use the scissors to cut out the mouth hole you just marked.

4. To cut out the features:

a. Trace the Face Half-Pattern using the Transfer Method (see page 15).

b. Cut one of the large front panels out of the second paper bag. Fold this panel in half from top to bottom.

c. Line up the left edge of the traced pattern with the fold of the paper and transfer the pattern onto the paper.

d. Cut out the features. Be sure to cut through **both** pieces of the paper so that the mouth, nose, and brow are connected around the fold, as shown. The eyes will not be connected.

5. Glue the eyes and the mouth to the mask at their corners, as shown.

6. To attach the nose and eyebrows:

a. Put glue on the center of the nose and eyebrow piece, as shown on page 62. Glue the center of the nose and eyebrow to the face so that it is between the eye holes and roughly centered and straight.

b. When the glue at the center of the nose is dry (about 20 minutes), glue the left and right sides of the piece, as shown on the pattern.

7. Your mask is ready to go. Slip it on and pretend you are a creature from outer space.

Face Half-Pattern

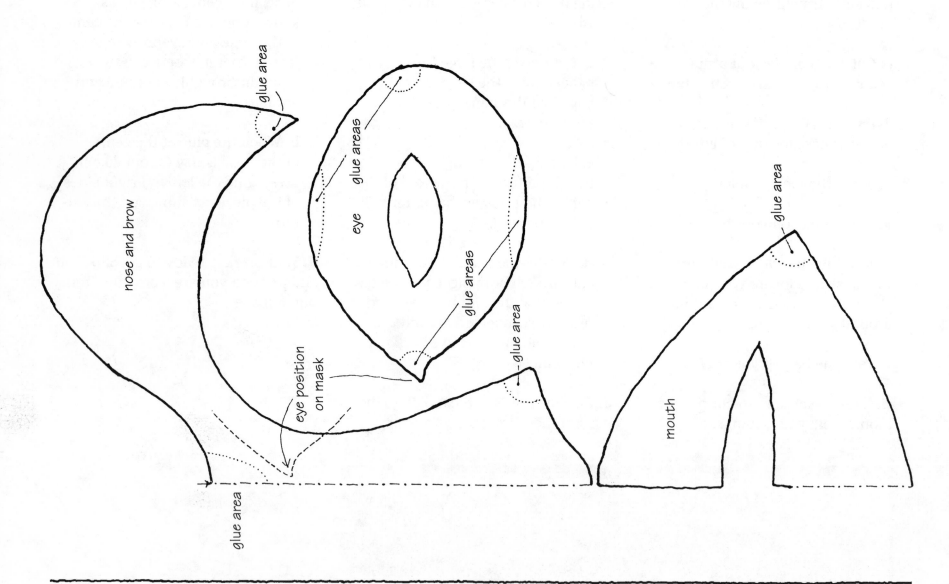

nose and brow

glue area

eye   glue areas

eye

glue areas

glue area

eye position
on mask

glue area

mouth

glue area

Plastic Masks

Instructions

1. Clean the jug inside and out and remove any labels.

a. Use the Pushpin Method (see page 14) and scissors to cut off the mouth of the jug just where it joins the body, as shown below.

2. Find the fine lines on the edges of the jug to the left and right of the handle. To make them easier to see, make pushpin holes every inch or so along the lines on the edges and on the bottom of the jug.

3. Cut the jug in half along the lines you have just marked. Use the Pushpin Method and scissors to make your cuts. The part of the jug with the handle is the "A" half and the other is the "B" half.

4. Use the scissors to round any sharp corners.

Bearded Lady Mask

You'll make this mask from the "A" half of the jug.

5. In order for you to see well through the mask, it is very important that you place the eye holes carefully. Find the right spacing for your eyes this way:

a. Put the half-jug upside down over your face. Hold it so that the tip of your nose rests in the hole at the bottom of the handle.

b. Hold the mask in place with one hand. Put the first and middle fingers of your other hand on the outside of the mask where your eyes are.

c. Keep your fingers in place. Carefully remove the mask from your face and put it down on your work surface. Have a friend mark around your fingers.

d. Use the marks as a guide to cut out eye holes $\frac{1}{2}$ inch (1.3 cm) in diameter (or larger), using the Pushpin Method.

e. Place the mask on your face to check that you can see well. Enlarge the eye holes if you have to. Don't worry if they turn out odd-looking.

Cut off the mouth around here.

"A" half of the jug (Bearded Lady)

"B" half of the jug (Robot)

Cut along this line to make the horn.

Cut along this indentation and remove the jug bottom from the "B" half only.

6. Use the diagram on page 66 and the scissors to make a centered "horn" on the top of the mask.

7. Punch a hole at either edge of the mask, just above the eye holes. Tie a short piece of string to each of the holes to hold the mask on your head.

8. Make five holes on both sides of the upper lip with your hole punch, as indicated on the diagram on page 66.

9. To make the beard:

   a. Tear eight pieces of fabric about 1 inch (2.5 cm) wide. Start the tears with small scissor-cuts, then rip the rest of the length. Tear a ninth piece of fabric about 4 inches (10 cm) wide and set it aside.

   b. Use the scissors to trim one end of each 1-inch (2.5-cm) strip into a point about 2 inches (5 cm) long.

   c. Pull the pointed end of each narrow strip through a hole (from front to back) far enough to tie a knot at the end. Do not tie strips through the two holes closest to the mouth.

   d. Pull all the strips down until the knots catch against the openings.

   e. For the holes nearest the mouth, take the 4-inch (10-cm) piece of fabric you set aside in step **9a** and make two cuts into one end of the fabric. Each cut should be about $1/4$ inch (.6 cm) from each side edge and about 2 inches (5 cm) long.

   f. Place one of the pieces you just cut in each of the holes nearest the mouth. Make a knot in each.

10. Use the diagram on page 66 as a guide to decorate the Bearded Lady Mask. Cut paper shapes and color them black and red. Use stick glue to glue them in place.

Robot Mask

You'll make this mask from the "B" half of the jug.

11. Put the second half of the jug over your face (again upside down) with your chin touching at the bottom.

   a. Use the scissors to cut off the bottom (now the top, since it's upside down) of the "B" half of the jug, as shown on page 64.

   b. Place the eye holes, as in step **5.** This mask will be a robot so make these eye holes rectangular.

12. Using the diagram on page 67, cut out the nostril holes, string holes, and the mouth hole.

13. Tie a piece of string through each of the holes on either side of the mask to hold the mask on your head.

14. Use the diagram on page 67 to decorate the mask with paper shapes, as in step **10**.

✪ **Even Better:** The Robot looks very good if you wear it with a black swim-cap.

Bearded Lady Decoration Guide
(not full size)

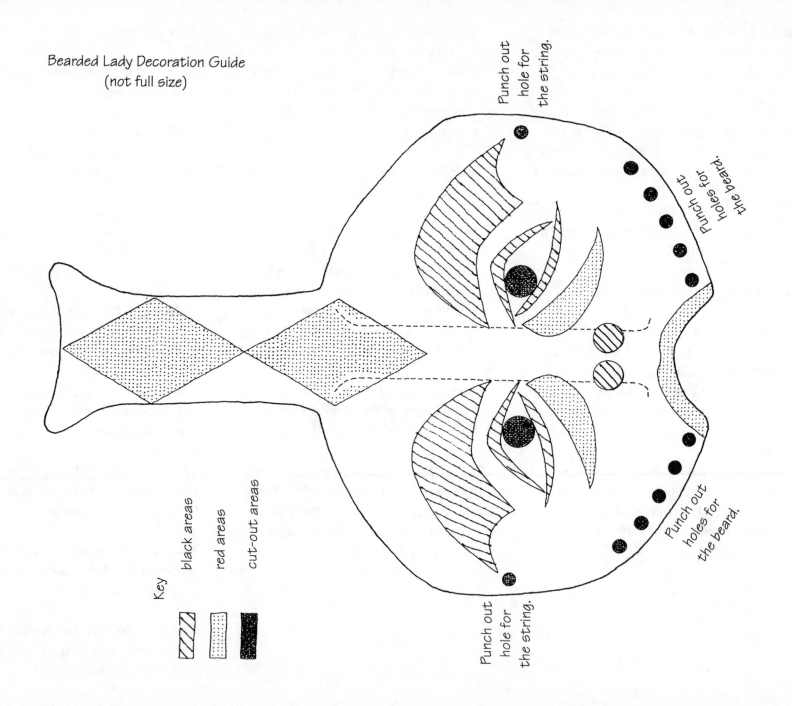

Punch out hole for the string.

Punch out holes for the beard.

Punch out holes for the beard.

Punch out hole for the string.

Key

black areas

red areas

cut-out areas

Robot Decoration Guide
(not full size)

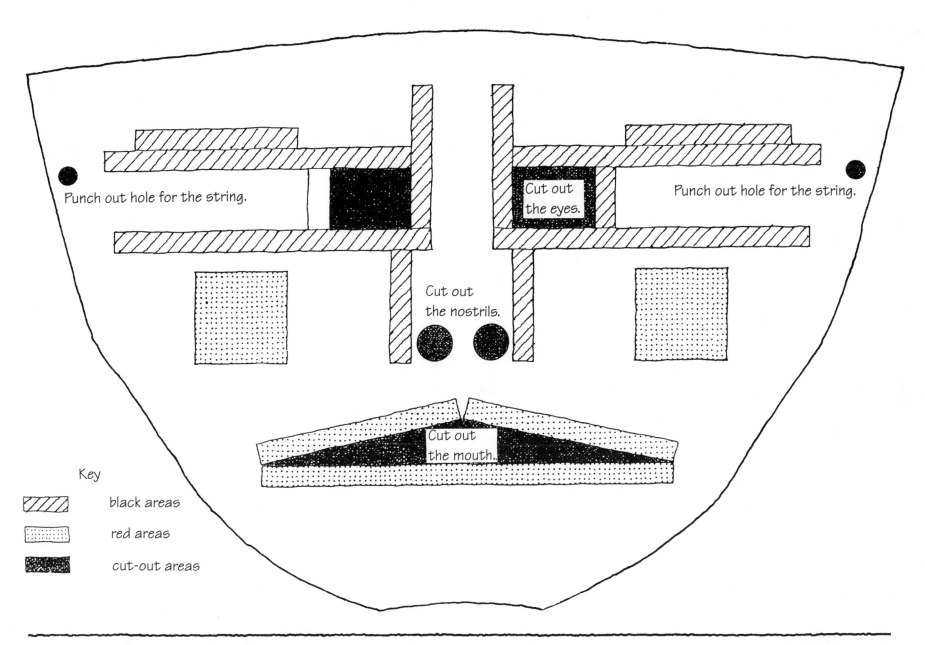

Punch out hole for the string.

Cut out the eyes.

Punch out hole for the string.

Cut out the nostrils.

Cut out the mouth.

Key

black areas

red areas

cut-out areas

Newspaper Puppet

Here's a way to make an old newspaper into a puppet.
You can give a newspaper puppet any personality you like.
We've chosen an old man to get you started.

You Need

☐ a page from a newspaper

Have on Hand

☐ a black marking pen
☐ stick glue

Tools

☐ scissors

Instructions

1. Turn the newspaper page sideways.

2. Fold it in half from side to side.

3. Fold the page in thirds from side to side.

4. Fold the page in half from top to bottom so that you now have two long folds.

5. Fold each section in half from bottom to top (the loose ends come up to meet the folded end) so that you have four sections. Crease all of these folds carefully with your finger.

6. Open up the newspaper so that it is only folded in half. Turn the newspaper over so that you are looking at the back of the page. You will draw the puppet's face on this side.

7. Draw and cut out the features of the puppet as shown on the facing page.

   a. In the top, center panel draw the eyes, nose, and upper lip. Cut out the nose and upper lip, but leave the bottom parts attached to the paper at the fold line, as shown.

   b. In the next panel down, draw the upper teeth. Cut them most of the way out, but again leave some of the top parts attached to the paper at the fold line.

   c. In the next panel down, draw the tongue and the lower teeth. Cut them out carefully, leaving the base of the tongue and the bottom of the teeth attached to the paper at the fold line.

   d. In the bottom section draw the lower lip and chin. Cut out only the bottom part of the lower lip and chin, leaving them attached at the fold lines.

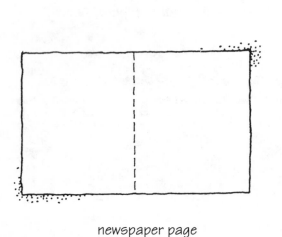

newspaper page

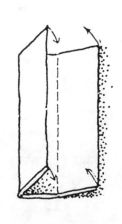

Fold in half.

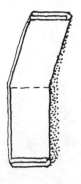

Fold in thirds.

Fold in half lengthwise.

Fold the two halves out toward the top.

e. Draw an ear and an eyebrow in each of the top side panels.

f. Cut the eyebrows out, leaving "stems" attached so that you can fold them later.

g. Cut around the ears. Be sure to leave them attached to the sides of the head with stems.

8. Refold the newspaper into thirds.

a. Gently fold and crease the ears **out**, the eyebrows **up** and **over**, and the nose **down**.

Note: If you like, you can glue the tip of the nose to the face about $1/2$ inch (1.3 cm) down, so that it bulges out.

b. Fold the upper lip down and the upper teeth up. Fold the tongue, the lower teeth, and the lower lip all down. Lastly, fold the chin up.

9. Finish refolding the newspaper.

10. To make the mouth open and close, put your thumb in the bottom pocket at the back and two or three fingers in the top pocket.

11. If the folds are too loose, you can use a little glue to keep them from coming undone. Be careful not to glue shut the pockets for your fingers.

✪ **Even Better:** Make a second puppet with a different face for your other hand so that the two puppets can talk to each other.

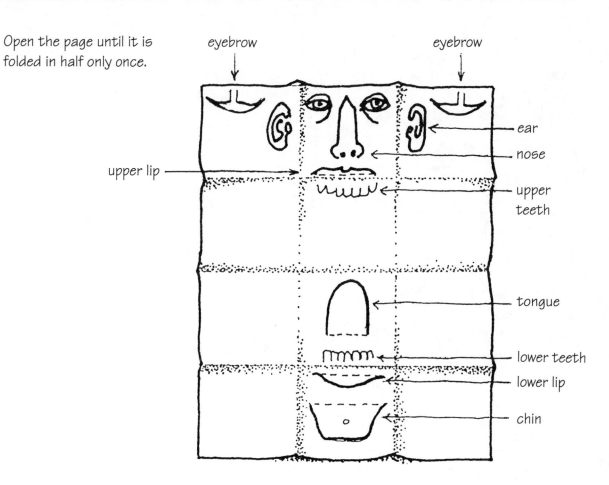

Open the page until it is folded in half only once.

eyebrow

eyebrow

ear

nose

upper lip

upper teeth

tongue

lower teeth

lower lip

chin

Two Kazoos

You can make sweet music with these two kinds of kazoo.
It's never hard to find old toilet-paper tubes,
and they have a million uses.

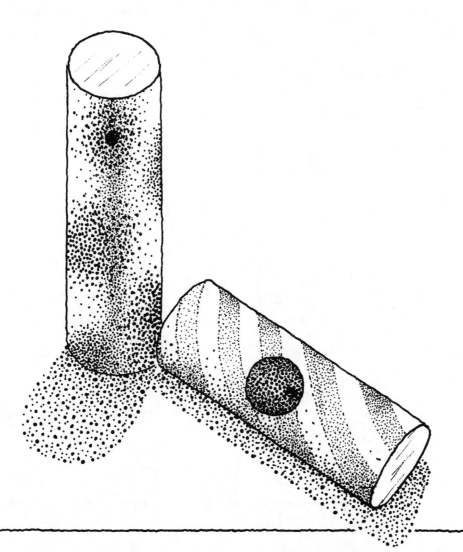

You Need

- ☐ two empty toilet-paper tubes
- ☐ thin paper (such as tracing paper, writing paper, or newspaper)

Have on Hand

- ☐ white glue

Tools

- ☐ a quarter
- ☐ a hole-punch
- ☐ a pushpin
- ☐ scissors

Instructions

1. If the ends of the toilet-paper tubes are loose, glue them into place.

2. Make air-escape holes by punching one hole in the side of each tube with the hole punch, as far from the end as the punch will reach.

3. Label one tube #1 and the other #2.

4. Using the quarter as a guide, draw a circle in the middle of tube #2, on the opposite side from the hole you punched in step **2**. Cut out the circle using the Pushpin Method (see page 14).

5. Cut three squares of paper large enough to cover one end of your tube.

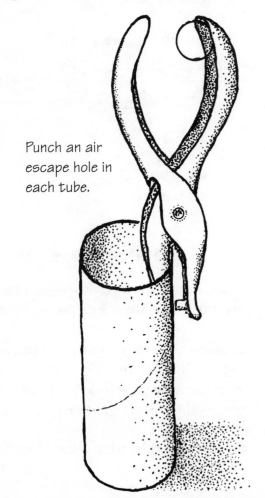

Punch an air escape hole in each tube.

6. Coat the edge of one end of tube #1 with white glue. Place the glued edge down firmly onto a square of paper. Leave the tube standing on the paper until the glue is completely dry (at least 20 minutes.)

7. Coat both ends of tube #2 with glue and attach the other two squares of paper in the same way.

8. When the glue has dried, use the scissors to trim the paper as close to the sides of the tubes as you can.

9. Put your mouth against the open end of Kazoo #1 and hum. When you

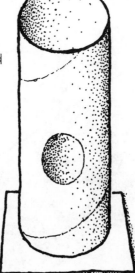

Glue paper to one end of tube #1 and both ends of tube #2.

hum into your Kazoos, let your lips vibrate as much as possible. Now try Kazoo #2, but in this case put your mouth over the quarter-sized hole in the side.

✪ **Even Better:** You can decorate your Kazoos any way you want. Try using paint, crayons, magic markers, or colored pencils.

Recycling Facts & Tips

Did you know that:

- It takes 17 trees to make 1 ton (.9 t) of paper.

How you can help:

- Use both sides of your paper. You can use the back of a half-used piece for drawing, notes, or anything.

Bang-a-Can Can

*You can make a drum just by tapping the end of an old
tin can with a pencil or stick. But your drum will
sound even better if you put some legs under it.*

You Need

- ☐ a cardboard box with sides at least 2 inches (5.1 cm) wide (such as a cereal box)
- ☐ a tin can with one end removed

❗ **Note:** Have an **adult helper** make sure there are no sharp edges left around the open end of the can.

Have on Hand

- ☐ pencils, pens, or sticks (to use as drumsticks)

Tools

- ☐ a pencil
- ☐ a ruler
- ☐ scissors

Instructions

1. Open the top and bottom flaps of the cardboard box. Cut the flaps off one end with the scissors. Flatten the box.

2. From the end with no flaps, measure and draw a line 1 inch (2.5 cm) up from, and parallel to, the end of the box, as shown below.

3. Cut off the strip you have just marked.

4. Measure and mark a line 2 inches (5 cm) from each side of the strip. Cut across the strip at these two marks so that you have two corners.

5. In the middle of each flattened corner, cut a centered slot $\frac{1}{2}$ inch (1.3 cm) deep. The slots should be about $\frac{1}{8}$ inch (.3 cm) wide.

6. Slip the two corners over the edge of the open end of the can. Place the corners opposite each other so the can balances.

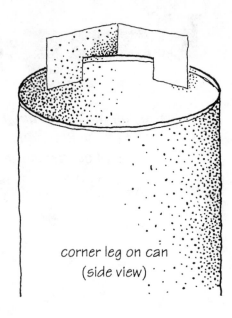

corner leg on can
(side view)

7. Turn the can over to stand on its legs. (For larger cans, use three or four legs, spacing them evenly around the can.)

8. Your drum is ready to roll. Use pencils, pens, or sticks to beat on your Bang-a-Can Can.

✪ **Even Better:** Make more drums from different-sized cans. Different cans will make different sounds.

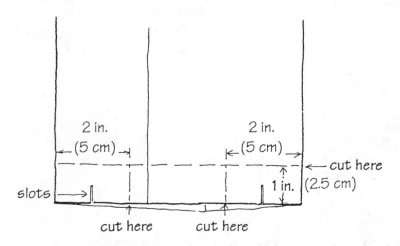

Keep the box flat for all cutting.

Juice-Can Stilts

Did you ever wish you were taller? These stilts are just the thing, and a couple of juice cans won't end up in the trash.

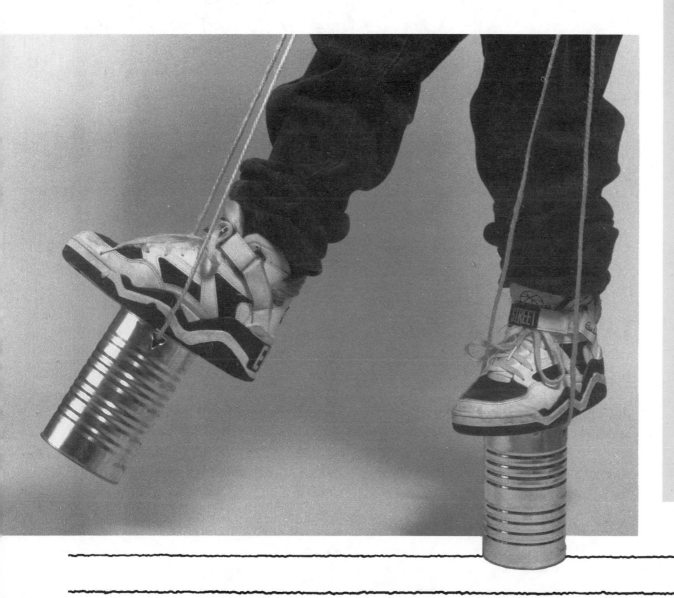

You Need

☐ two clean, empty juice cans that are 7 inches high and 4 inches in diameter (17.8 cm high and 10 cm in diameter) with both ends still on

Note: Do not use juice cans that have open ends. Use cans that have been opened with small holes.

☐ two pieces of rope that are each 48 inches (1.2 m) or longer

Have on Hand

☐ masking tape

Tools

☐ a juice can opener (the kind that has a triangular punch at one end)
☐ a long knitting needle

Instructions

1. Stand one can upside down on your work surface. Use the can opener to make two triangular openings opposite each other in the **sides** of the can, as shown below.

juice can opener

Make openings on both sides of the can.

2. Tape the end of one piece of rope to the pointed end of the knitting needle.

3. Carefully push the knitting needle, with the rope attached, through the two holes that you made in step **1**.

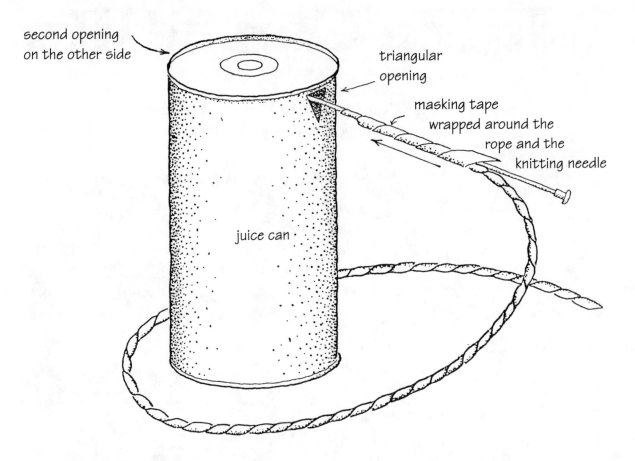

second opening on the other side

triangular opening

masking tape wrapped around the rope and the knitting needle

juice can

4. Slide the knitting needle all the way through. Untape the rope and tie the ends together.

5. Repeat steps **1** through **4** for the second can.

6. While holding the ropes, place one foot on each can. To walk, use the rope to pull the can against the bottom of your foot as you take a step.

Note: Do not use your stilts indoors, because they might damage the floor.

7. If it's hard to walk, try making the ropes longer or shorter to suit your height.

Things for Fun

Balancing Toy

Can you make an old file folder balance on your finger?
We'll show you how. Once you've put this toy together,
you'll have a hard time tipping it over.

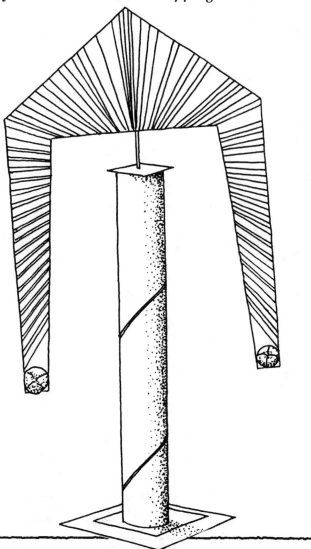

Instructions

Note: The measurements and cuts you make for this project must be **exact**, or the toy won't balance.

1. Make the following measurements and cuts on the file folder. Keep the file folder closed while you cut, and be sure to cut through both sides together so that they are the same.

a. Use the ruler and the pencil to make marks on the top and bottom of the folder $8\frac{1}{4}$ inches (21 cm) from the fold, as shown at right. Draw a line connecting these two marks.

b. Make marks on both the fold edge and the open edge $\frac{1}{2}$ inch (1.3 cm) up from the bottom. Draw a line connecting these two marks.

c. Use the scissors to cut along these two lines.

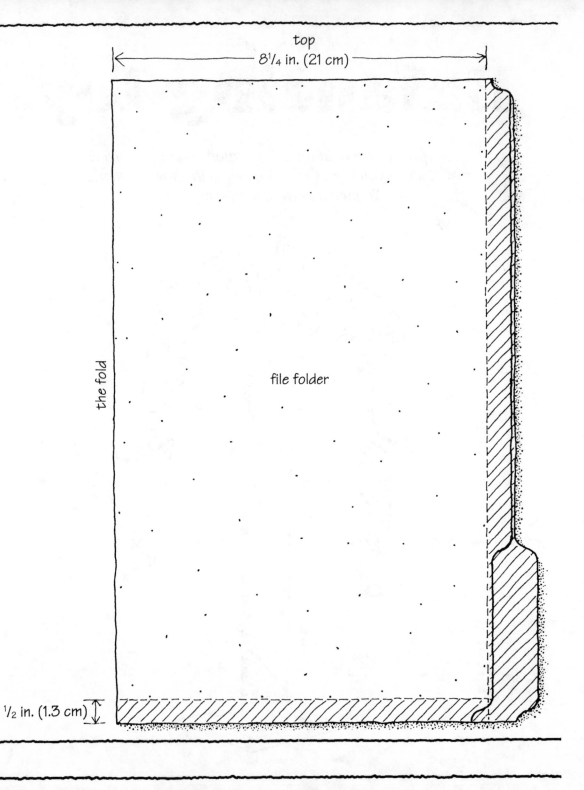

top
$8\frac{1}{4}$ in. (21 cm)

the fold

file folder

$\frac{1}{2}$ in. (1.3 cm)

d. Use the ruler and the pencil to measure and mark the dimensions, as shown at right. First make the marks, then draw the lines.

e. Use the scissors to cut along the lines you have just drawn.

2. To position the balancing stick:

a. Open the folder. Use the Measuring and Marking Method (see page 12) to find and mark the center of the arch on one of the inside faces of the folder.

b. Use the pencil and the ruler to draw a line from the center of the arch up to the center point at the top of the folder.

c. Break 1 inch (2.5 cm) off the end of a straight shish-kebab skewer, so that it is 5 inches (12.7 cm) long. (Ask an **adult** for help if you need it.)

d. Trail white glue along the skewer, except for 1 inch (2.5 cm) at one end.

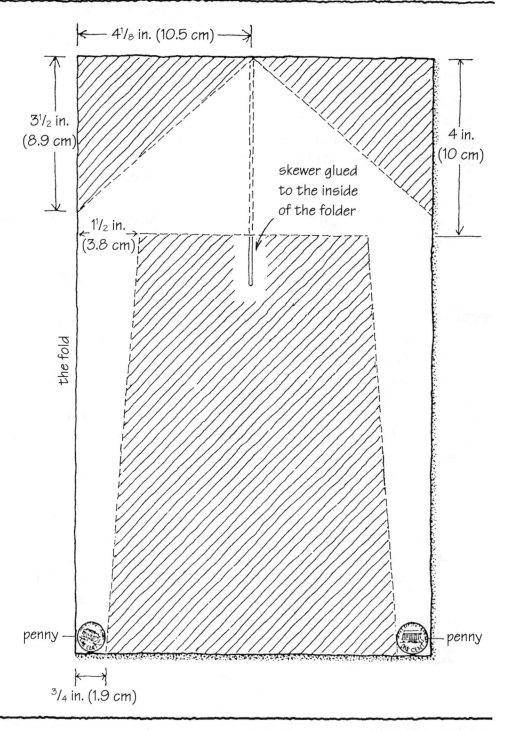

4¹⁄₈ in. (10.5 cm)

3¹⁄₂ in. (8.9 cm)

4 in. (10 cm)

skewer glued to the inside of the folder

1¹⁄₂ in. (3.8 cm)

the fold

penny

penny

³⁄₄ in. (1.9 cm)

e. Place the skewer on the guide-line you have just drawn. The 1-inch (2.5-cm) portion without glue should stick out into the arch. Wipe off any extra glue.

f. Place the unopened can on top of the skewer to hold it in place while it dries. Wait until the glue is completely dry (at least 20 minutes) before going on to the next step.

3. To glue the folder closed:

a. Apply stick glue all over the inside of the folder, especially near the edges.

b. Trail white glue along the top side of the skewer, except the part that is sticking down from the folder.

c. Close the folder and press it together from the folded edge to the open edge. Place the can on the closed folder where the skewer is positioned. Wait at least 20 minutes for the glue to dry before going on to the next step.

4. When the glue has dried, use several pieces of double-sided tape to stick a penny at the bottom of both sides of each leg.

5. To make the stand:

a. Attach one end of the paper-towel tube to the center of the 4-inch (10-cm) square of cardboard with white glue. Wait at least 20 minutes for the glue to dry before going on to the next step.

b. Attach the other end of the paper-towel tube to the center of the 1³/₄-inch (4.4-cm) square of cardboard using white glue. Wait at least 20 minutes for the glue to dry before going on to the next step.

6. Your Balancing Toy is ready. Just place the end of the skewer on the top of the stand or on your finger and it will balance. If it doesn't balance, try moving the pennies slightly up and down until their weight is even.

Recycling Facts & Tips

Did you know that:

- The U. S. throws away 500,000 tons (450,000 t) of trash every day.

- This much trash would fill nearly 92 million lunchboxes!

How you can help:

- Wrap your sandwich in aluminum foil, which can be recycled, not in plastic wrap, which can't.

- Bring drinks to school in a thermos, rather than in disposable containers like juice packs or cans.

Tin-Can Telephone

Yes, this telephone really works, and you can reuse any two tin cans to make it.

You Need

☐ two tin cans, each with one end removed

❗ **Note:** Have an **adult helper** make sure there are no sharp edges left around the open ends of the cans.

☐ 20 feet (6 m) of string

Note: Heavy string or twine will **not** work well.

Have on Hand

☐ one friend

Tools

❗ a hammer
❗ a small nail

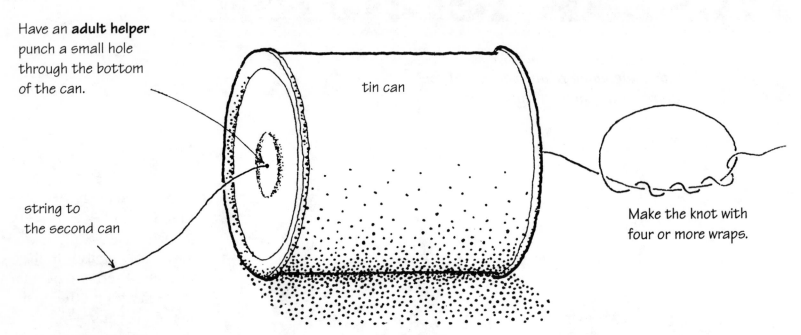

Have an **adult helper** punch a small hole through the bottom of the can.

tin can

string to the second can

Make the knot with four or more wraps.

Instructions

1. Make sure that your cans are clean and that any paper labels have been removed.

!2. Stand the cans on a flat surface with their open ends down. Have an **adult helper** punch a small hole through the centers of the bottoms of both cans with the nail and hammer. The hole should be just large enough for the end of the string to pass through it.

3. Pull an end of the string through the hole in each can.

4. Tie a knot in each end of the string, as shown above. The knots should be large enough that they will not pull through the holes.

5. Hold one can and have your friend hold the other. Stretch the string as far as it will go. Have your friend hold the open end of one can to his or her ear while you talk into the open end of the other.

6. The phones will work best when the string is pulled tight and straight.

Construction Kit

*You can make forms and shapes out of used
Styrofoam trays to create nearly anything—buildings,
machines, even prehistoric monsters.*

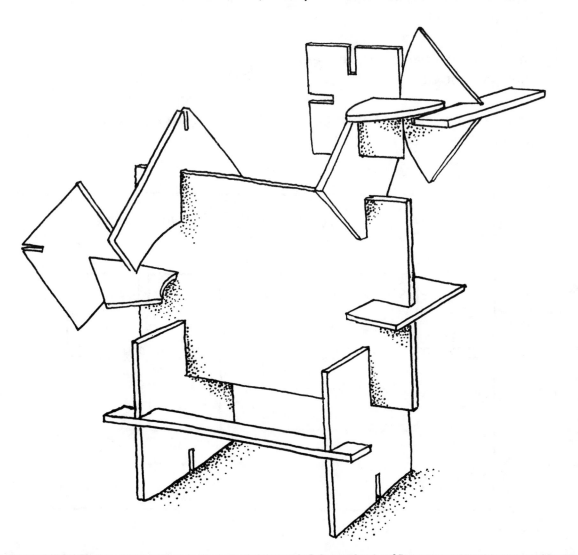

You Need

- ☐ Styrofoam meat or produce trays (as many as you can find)

Have on Hand

- ☐ tracing paper (or any paper you can see through)
- ☐ white glue

Tools

- ☐ a pencil
- ☐ scissors

Instructions

1. Make sure the Styrofoam trays are clean and dry.

2. Cut off the curved edges all around so that the trays are flat and the corners are roughly square.

3. You can make construction pieces of any size and shape. Any piece you make will need slots to connect it to other pieces. Make the slots like this:

a. Use the tip of the scissors to make two cuts that are about ¹/₂ to ³/₄ inch (1.3-1.9 cm) long and about ¹/₁₆ inch (.2 cm) apart. You don't have to measure, just cut by sight.

b. Carefully break out the material between the cuts.

c. It's OK if some slots are bigger and some smaller.

4. Look below for some sample shapes. Use the Transfer Method (see page 15) to trace the shapes onto a Styrofoam tray. Cut the shapes out and you can make anything you want.

✪ **Even Better:** You can decorate your construction pieces with glued-on paper patterns.

Suggested Construction Shapes

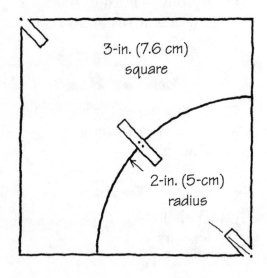

3-in. (7.6 cm) square

2-in. (5-cm) radius

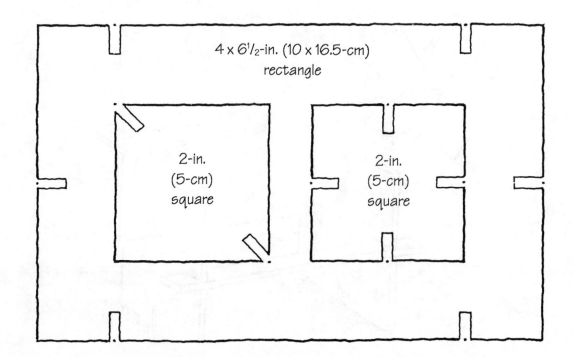

4 x 6¹/₂-in. (10 x 16.5-cm) rectangle

2-in. (5-cm) square

2-in. (5-cm) square

Nodosaurid

The Nodosaurid Polacantus is made of recycled Styrofoam trays, just like the Construction Kit on page 87.

You Need

- [ ] light cardboard (such as from a cereal box)
- [ ] several Styrofoam meat or produce trays
- [ ] white scrap paper

Have on Hand

- [ ] masking tape
- [ ] stick glue
- [ ] tracing paper
- [ ] white glue

Tools

- [ ] a pencil
- [ ] scissors

Instructions

1. Use the Transfer Method (see page 15) to trace the patterns from the next two pages onto pieces of cardboard:

a. Trace only up to the joint marks on the Front Body Pattern.

b. Line the tracing up with the joint marks on the Tail Pattern and continue tracing.

c. Transfer the patterns to the cardboard.

2. Transfer to cardboard one of each pattern, except for the B, C, and D horns (see page 92). Transfer four each of these.

3. Cut out the pattern pieces with scissors.

a. It's a good idea to label the pattern pieces before you cut them out, so you will know later which part is which.

4. Use scissors to trim the curved edges off the Styrofoam trays.

5. If your piece of Styrofoam is not long enough to fit the whole dinosaur body, you can join two pieces.

a. Find two pieces of Styrofoam that the dinosaur pattern will fit on.

b. Glue the two pieces together with stick glue.

c. Glue a piece of scrap paper along the line where the two pieces meet.

d. Repeat step **c** on the other side where the two pieces meet.

6. To cut out the body parts from the Styrofoam trays:

a. Hold a cardboard pattern piece down flat on the Styrofoam and draw around the edges of the patterns several times with a sharp pencil.

b. When the pattern is clearly outlined, cut it out with the scissors.

c. Cut out the slots, as shown in the patterns.

7. To assemble the Nodosaurid:

a. Place the back leg slot into the rear body slot.

b. Place the front leg slot into the front body slot and stand the Nodosaurid on its feet.

c. Place the horns in their slots, according to the letters indicated on the pattern (A, B, C, etc.).

d. If any of the horns are loose, use a drop of white glue to hold them in place.

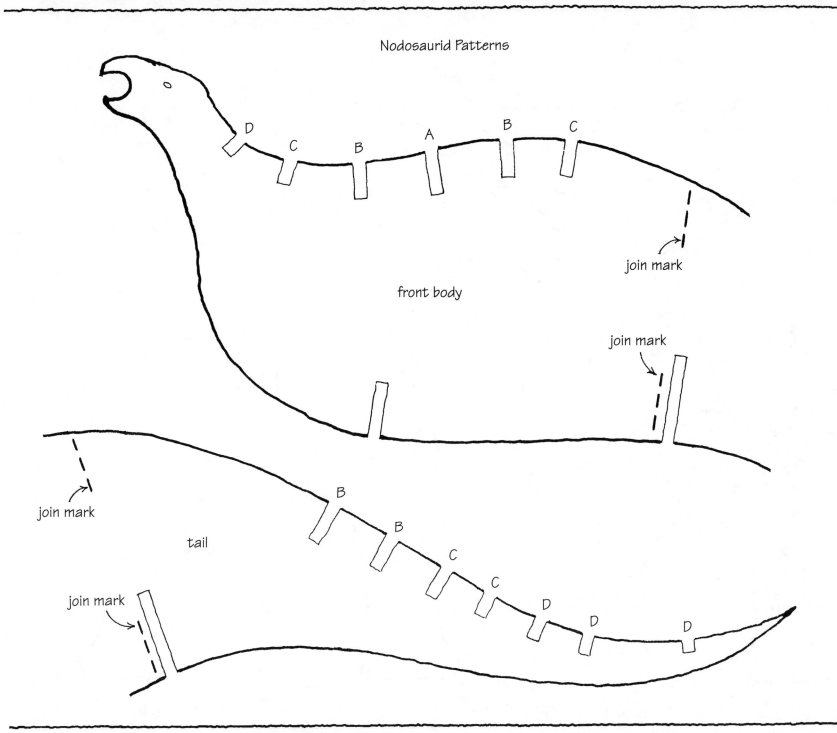

front body

join mark

join mark

tail

join mark

join mark

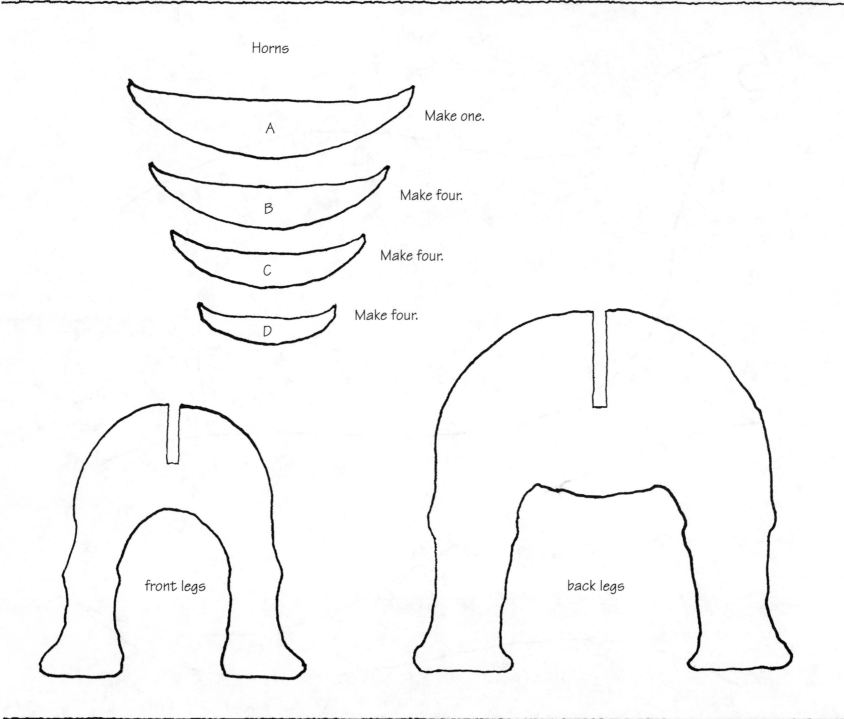

Horns

A Make one.

B Make four.

C Make four.

D Make four.

front legs

back legs

Twister

The Twister creates an optical illusion—it makes you think that two pictures become one. To make the Twister, you will reuse an old playing card and some used paper.

You Need

- [ ] a playing card (use one from a deck that is worn out or not complete)
- [ ] white paper to cover both sides of the card (use the second side of paper that has already been used once)
- [ ] two 12-inch (30.5-cm) pieces of string

Have on Hand

- [ ] black poster paint
- [ ] marking pens in lots of colors
- [ ] newspaper
- [ ] stick glue

Tools

- [ ] a paintbrush
- [ ] a pencil
- [ ] a pushpin
- [ ] a ruler

Instructions

1. Cover your work area with newspaper.

2. Paint one side of the playing card with black poster paint to cover the pattern. Wait at least 20 minutes for the paint to dry.

3. Paint the other side of the card. Wait at least 20 minutes for the paint to dry before going on to the next step.

4. Use the scissors to cut two pieces of paper a little larger than the card.

5. Rub stick glue on one piece of paper (the used side) and on one side of the card.

6. Stick the paper to the card.

7. Use the scissors to trim any extra paper from around the edges of the card.

8. Glue the second piece of paper to the card and trim away any extra paper.

9. Draw a bird on one side of the card. You can copy the bird shown here or you can draw your own.

10. Draw the bars on the other side of the card, as show in the drawing on the opposite page.

Note: The Twister will work best if the bird is in bright colors like yellow, pink, or blue and the cage is in dark colors like brown or black.

11. Use the Measuring and Marking Method (see page 12) to find and mark the center points on the top and bottom of the card.

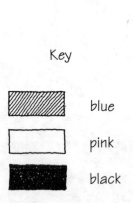

Key

blue

pink

black

12. Use the pushpin to punch holes about ¼ inch (.6 cm) in from the marks you made in step **10**.

13. Enlarge the holes with the point of the pencil so that they are large enough to thread a piece of string through.

14. Thread one piece of string through each hole. Tie a knot to fix the string to the card.

15. To make the card twist:

a. Holding each string with the thumb and first finger of each hand, roll the string back and forth.

b. As you twirl the card, watch what happens. The bird will "jump" into the cage.

Recycling Facts & Tips

Did you know that:

- More than 13 million tons (11.7 million t) of glass are made in the United States each year. Almost all of that glass is made into containers for food and drinks.

- Glass can be recycled again and again. Unlike plastic, which can only be recycled a few times, glass can be recycled as many times as people want to recycle it.

How you can help:

- We are already recycling nearly one quarter of the glass containers we use.

- Each 1-liter glass bottle that you recycle saves enough energy to light a light bulb for 4 hours.

Cloth Doll

This doll is fun to make from old fabric. It will fit easily in the cradle that you can make in the next project.

You Need

- [ ] one 8 × 10-inch (20 × 25-cm) piece of light-colored cloth
- [ ] one 8 × 10-inch (20 × 25-cm) piece of light cardboard
- [ ] two handfuls of cotton balls

Have on Hand

- [ ] marking pens
- [ ] newspaper
- [ ] sewing thread
- [ ] white glue
- [ ] tracing paper
- [ ] two fine, felt-tipped writing pens (one black, one green)

Tools

- [ ] a needle with a large eye
- [ ] a pencil with an eraser
- [ ] a ruler
- [ ] scissors

Instructions

1. Use the Transfer Method (see page 15) to transfer the Doll Outline Pattern on this page to the cardboard.

    a. Cut out the pattern with scissors.

    b. Mark the "front" side and the "back" side of the pattern.

2. Use the ruler and the pencil to draw a line 1 inch (2.5 cm) up from the long side of the fabric, as shown on the opposite page. This is line #1.

    a. Measure and mark the center point on line #1, 5 inches (12.7 cm) in from both sides.

    b. Mark the center point on the top of the fabric, 5 inches (12.7 cm) in from both sides.

    c. Use the ruler and pencil to draw a line connecting these two points. This is line #2.

Doll-Outline Pattern

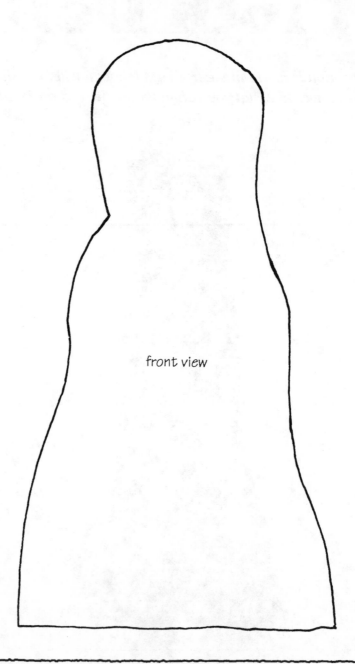

front view

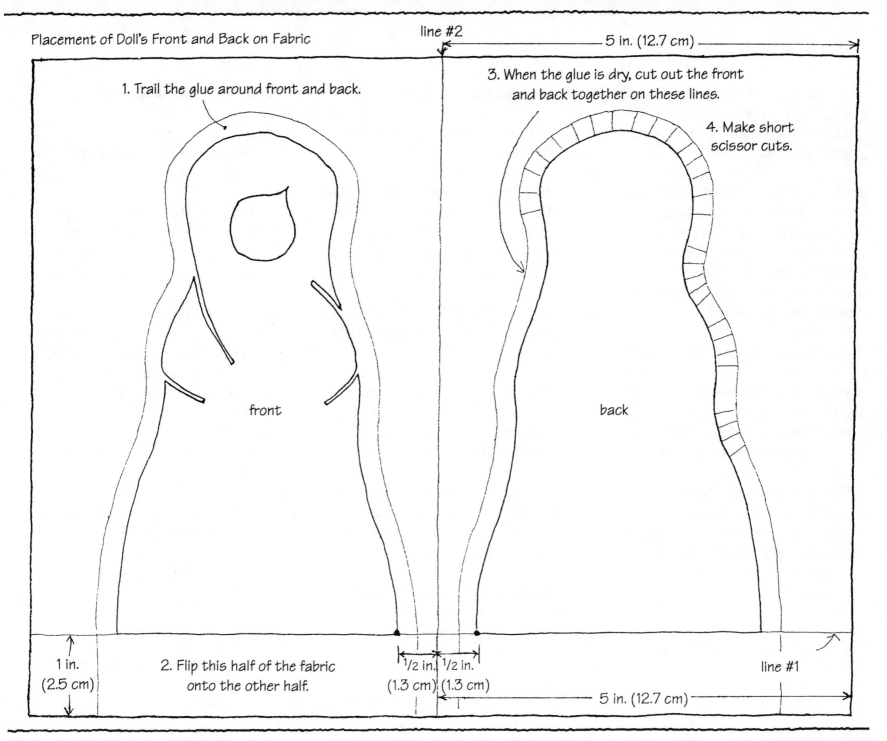

Placement of Doll's Front and Back on Fabric

line #2

5 in. (12.7 cm)

1. Trail the glue around front and back.

3. When the glue is dry, cut out the front and back together on these lines.

4. Make short scissor cuts.

front

back

1 in. (2.5 cm)

2. Flip this half of the fabric onto the other half.

½ in. (1.3 cm)   ½ in. (1.3 cm)

line #1

5 in. (12.7 cm)

d. Use the ruler and pencil to make marks on line #1 exactly ¹/₂ inch (1.3 cm) on either side of where line #1 crosses line #2.

3. Line up the cardboard Doll Outline Pattern, "front" up, on the left half of the fabric. The bottom of the pattern should rest on line #1 and the right edge of the pattern at the mark you made in step **2d**. Trace around the pattern with the pencil.

4. Flip the pattern over and place it on the right side of the fabric. The bottom of the pattern should rest on line #1 and the left edge of the pattern at the other mark you made in step **2d**. Trace around the pattern with the pencil.

5. Decorate the doll's front and back following the design on the next page, or make your own design. Draw the face with a fine, black pen.

6. To put the doll together:

  a. Cover your work area with newspaper.

  b. Trail glue around the edges of the doll's front and back. Do **not** glue along the **bottom**. Try to trail the glue about ¹/₈ inch (.3 cm) away from the edge of the pattern.

  c. Carefully fold the two patterns together face-to-face. Line up the edges of the fabric.

  d. Press the halves together on the newspaper. Wait at least 30 minutes for the glue to dry before going on to the next step.

7. Use the scissors to cut around the sides (but not the bottom) of the doll. Cut roughly ¹/₄ inch (.64 cm) away from the edge of the glue.

8. Make short scissor cuts around the top and side of the doll, as shown on the previous page.

9. To turn the doll inside out:

  a. Thread the needle and tie the two ends of the thread together with a large knot.

  b. Insert the needle through the top of the head, so that the point of the needle is inside the doll, between the two pieces of fabric.

  c. Open up the two pieces of fabric from the bottom and carefully pull the needle out through the bottom of the doll. Be sure that the needle doesn't go through any more of the fabric.

  d. Cut the thread to remove the needle.

  e. Pull on the thread and gently turn the doll right-side out.

  f. Remove the thread.

Guide for Decorating the
Doll's Front and Back

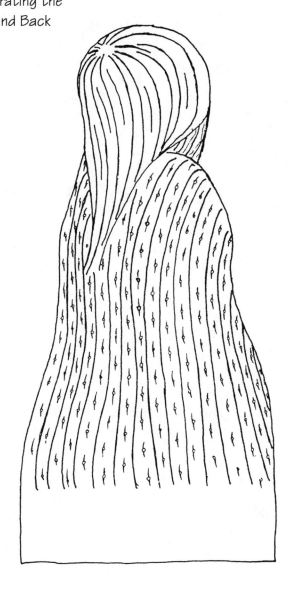

10. Use the pencil to stuff wads of absorbent cotton into the doll. Small pieces are easier to put in than large ones. Use the eraser end of the pencil to help push cotton into all the spaces. Stop filling the doll while it is still easy to close the bottom.

11. Glue the bottom of the doll closed by trailing glue along the inside of the doll, where the edges of the pattern are, and pressing the two pieces together. Wait at least 30 minutes for the glue to dry.

12. When the glue is dry, use the scissors to trim off the extra fabric.

13. Use the marking pens to decorate the bottom of the Cloth Doll and to touch up the edges.

✪ **Even Better:** If you use sand or dried beans to fill the doll, instead of absorbent cotton, she will stand up by herself.

Cradle

Oatmeal and ice cream don't usually go together, but their old containers make a cradle any doll would envy.

You Need

- [ ] one oatmeal carton with a plastic lid
- [ ] one cardboard lid from a ½-gallon (2-liter) drum-shaped ice-cream container

Have on Hand

- [ ] a pencil
- [ ] a permanent marking pen with a fine point
- [ ] a sheet of typing paper
- [ ] white glue

Tools

- [ ] a pushpin
- [ ] scissors
- [ ] sewing scissors
- [ ] a ruler

Instructions

1. Cut a strip of paper about 2½ inches (6.4 cm) wide and at least 13 inches (33 cm) long.

2. Wrap the strip of paper around the oatmeal carton. Make a mark on the paper where it overlaps. Use the scissors to cut off the short "tail" of paper after the mark. Discard the tail.

3. Fold the strip of paper in half. Now you have a piece of paper that fits exactly halfway around the carton.

4. To mark the two sides of the cradle, you must draw two lines on the oatmeal carton from top to bottom, as follows:

    a. Wrap the paper around the **top** of the carton. Line up one end of the paper with the carton's label. Make a pencil mark on the carton at the other end of the paper. Make a second mark in the same way at the **bottom** of the carton.

    b. To mark the first side, draw a line with the pencil and ruler connecting the two points you've just marked.

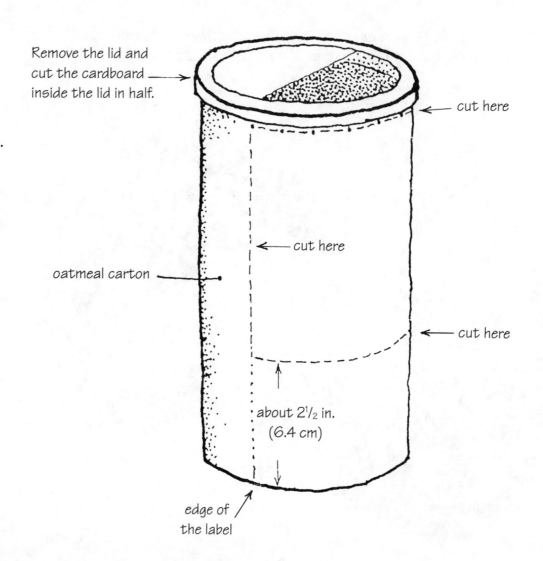

Remove the lid and cut the cardboard inside the lid in half.

cut here

cut here

oatmeal carton

cut here

about 2½ in. (6.4 cm)

edge of the label

c. For the second side, draw a pencil line down the edge of the label.

5. To mark the cradle hood:

a. Wrap the paper strip around the bottom of the carton.

b. Draw a line along the top of the strip to connect the two lines you drew in step **4.**

6. Use the Pushpin Method (see page 14) and sewing scissors to make the following cuts:

a. Cut the lines you drew in step **4.**

b. Remove the plastic lid from the oatmeal carton and cut around the top, starting and ending at the lines you drew in step **4.** It's probably easier to cut from the inside. There may be a reinforcing ring at the top that you can use as a guide for your cut.

c. Cut out half of the cardboard in the oatmeal carton lid, as shown. Replace the lid on the carton.

7. To make the rockers:

a. Place the ice-cream container lid upside down on your work surface.

b. Stand the oatmeal carton in the center of the ice-cream container lid.

c. Draw a line around the base of the oatmeal carton with a pen.

d. Cut the ice-cream lid in half with the scissors.

e. Use the scissors to cut out the half circles you drew in step **5c**.

8. To glue the rockers to the carton:

a. Apply glue to the inside edge of one rocker.

b. Stand the carton up. Push the glued edge of the rocker against the uncut half of the carton.

c. When the glue is dry, turn the carton on its other end and glue the other rocker in place.

9. When all the glue has dried, your Cradle is ready to rock.

✪ **Even Better:** You can decorate your Cradle any way you want. Try using crayons, markers, or glued-on paper shapes. Don't forget about the Cloth Doll on page 97; she'll fit perfectly into this cradle.

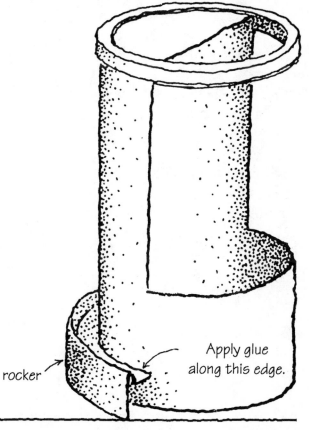

rocker

Apply glue along this edge.

The Castle

Our castle has a gate, a gatehouse, and towers, all made from previously used items such as oatmeal cartons, toilet-paper tubes, and a cookie box.

You Need

- [ ] two 42-ounce (1.2-kg) oatmeal cartons (5 inches [12.7 cm] in diameter)
- [ ] two 18-ounce (510-g) oatmeal cartons (4 inches [10 cm] in diameter)
- [ ] one cracker or cookie box about $9 \times 5 \times 2\frac{1}{4}$ inches ($22.9 \times 12.7 \times 5.7$ cm)
- [ ] three toilet-paper tubes
- [ ] two paper-towel tubes
- [ ] scraps of light cardboard (such as from a cereal box)

Have on Hand

- [ ] a black marking pen
- [ ] black poster paint
- [ ] white glue
- [ ] yellow glue

Tools

- [ ] a butter knife
- [ ] a pencil
- [ ] a pushpin
- [ ] a ruler
- [ ] scissors

Instructions

1. To make the towers:

a. Cut the metal or plastic reinforcing rings off the tops of the four oatmeal cartons, using the Pushpin Method (see page 14).

b. Use the Transfer Method (page 15) to copy the three Battlement Patterns onto three strips of light cardboard. Use the scissors to cut out the battlements from the strips.

c. Line up the tops of the cardboard patterns with the tops of the cartons and tubes. Draw around the patterns with a pencil to make the battlement shapes. The patterns don't fit all the way around, so move them as you need to. Be sure to line them up with marks you have already made.

Note: Use pattern A for the larger oatmeal cartons. Use pattern B for the smaller oatmeal cartons. Use pattern C for both the paper-towel and the toilet-paper tubes.

d. Use the Pushpin Method and scissors to cut out the battlements.

Battlement Patterns

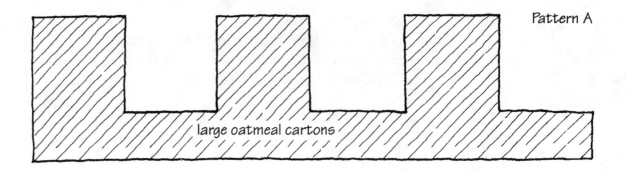

Pattern A

large oatmeal cartons

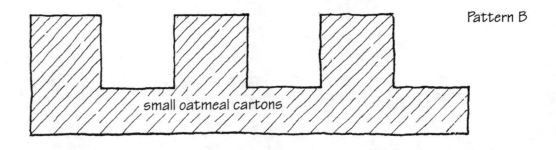

Pattern B

small oatmeal cartons

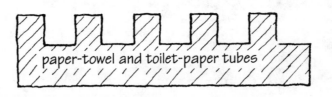

Pattern C

paper-towel and toilet-paper tubes

2. To make the small turrets:

a. Use the scissors to cut two slits straight up from the bottoms of two toilet-paper tubes. The slits should be ½ inch (1.3 cm) high and 1 inch (2.5 cm) apart.

b. Cut the third toilet-paper tube in half with the scissors. Discard one half. Cut two slits in the bottom of the shortened tube that are 2 inches (5 cm) high and 1 inch (2.5 cm) apart.

3. To make the large turrets:

a. Use the ruler and pencil to mark two vertical lines on the two paper-towel tubes from bottom to top and 1 inch (2.5 cm) apart.

b. Use the scissors to cut slits along these lines. Start at the bottom and cut up 7 inches (17.8 cm).

4. To make the gatehouse:

a. Cut off the top and bottom flaps of the cracker box with the scissors.

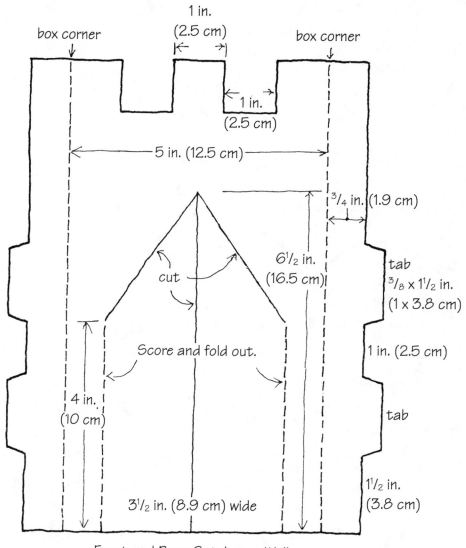

Front and Rear Gatehouse Wall

Castle Floor Plan

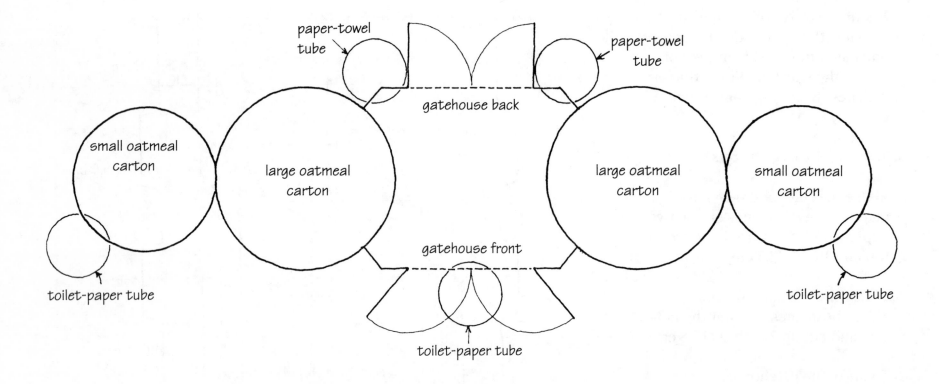

paper-towel tube

paper-towel tube

gatehouse back

small oatmeal carton

large oatmeal carton

large oatmeal carton

small oatmeal carton

gatehouse front

toilet-paper tube

toilet-paper tube

toilet-paper tube

b. Cut the box in half lengthwise, cutting up the middle of the side panels of the box.

c. Follow the diagram on the opposite page to mark and cut both pieces of the cracker box. Remember that you should **fold**, but not cut, the hinges on the castle doors.

5. To assemble the castle:

a. Fold in the tabs of the front and rear gatehouse walls. Cover their outer sides with glue and press them against the larger oatmeal cartons. Hold the tabs in place for a minute for the glue to set. Wait at least 20 minutes for the glue to dry before going on to the next step.

b. Glue the larger and smaller oatmeal cartons together, as shown in the floor-plan diagram. Hold the cartons together for a minute for the glue to set. Again, wait at least 20 minutes for the glue to dry before going on to the next step.

c. Slip the slit toilet-paper and paper-towel tubes over the walls of the castle in the positions shown.

6. Your Castle is complete.

✪ **Even Better:** You can make flags by cutting out long triangles of colored magazine paper and gluing them to toothpicks. You can also paint your Castle in any way you like.

Recycling Facts & Tips

Did you know that:

- In the United States, over 16 million tons (14.5 t) of plastic are made each year.

- Most plastics can only be recycled a few times before they break down too much to be used again.

How you can help:

- Even though some plastics can be recycled, plastics are far from being earth-friendly. It's best not to buy things packaged in plastic. (You can often buy the same thing in other packaging.) If you do buy plastic packaging, be sure that it gets recycled.

Games
to Play

Picture Puzzle

You can make your own picture puzzle out of an old cereal box and a magazine, but it's not as easy as it looks to put this puzzle back together.

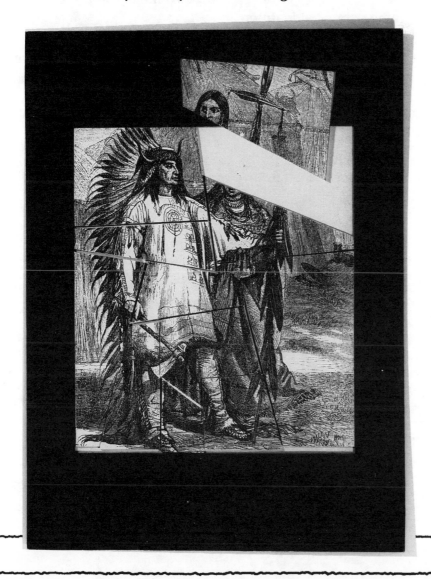

You Need

- ☐ two $7^1/_2 \times 10$-inch (19×25-cm) pieces of light cardboard (such as from a cereal box)
- ☐ two pictures (about $5^1/_2 \times 7^1/_2$ inches [14×19 cm]) cut from a magazine

Note: The pictures you pick should have very different colors and shapes in them.

Have on Hand

- ☐ black poster paint
- ☐ newspaper
- ☐ stick glue
- ☐ white glue

Tools

- ☐ a glue brush
- ☐ a pencil
- ☐ a pushpin
- ☐ a ruler
- ☐ scissors
- ☐ a small paintbrush

Instructions

1. To make the puzzle frame:

a. Mark a centered $5\frac{1}{2} \times 7\frac{1}{2}$-inch ($14 \times 19$-cm) rectangle on one piece of cardboard, using the Measuring and Marking Method (see page 12).

b. Use the Pushpin Method (see page 14) and scissors to cut out the rectangle. Cut very carefully and neatly because you will need the piece you cut out.

c. Once you have finished cutting the rectangle, cover your work area with newspaper.

d. Paint one side of the frame with black poster paint. Be sure to paint the edges too. Wait at least 20 minutes for the paint to dry before going on to the next step.

e. When the paint is dry, brush a light coat of glue over the paint to protect it. Wait at least 20 minutes for the glue to dry.

f. Once the glue has dried, brush another coat of glue on the unpainted side of the frame to prevent it from warping. Wait for the glue to dry before going on.

g. Lay the frame painted-side **down** on your work surface and apply stick glue to the unpainted side of the frame.

h. Place the second piece of cardboard on top of the frame. Be sure that all the edges line up.

i. Press down firmly to set the glue. Wait at least 20 minutes for the glue to dry. (You can go on to the next step while the glue is drying.)

2. To make the puzzle pieces:

a. Rub stick glue onto the back of one of the pictures and onto one side of the cardboard rectangle you cut out in step **1**.

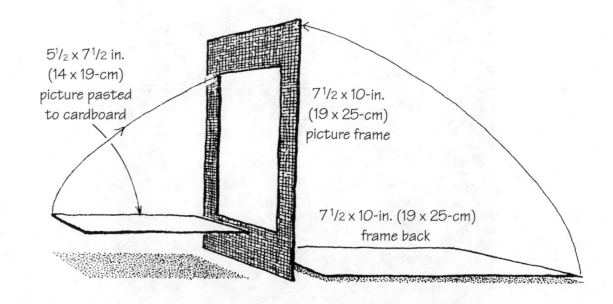

Assembly of the Puzzle

$5\frac{1}{2} \times 7\frac{1}{2}$ in. (14×19-cm) picture pasted to cardboard

$7\frac{1}{2} \times 10$-in. (19×25-cm) picture frame

$7\frac{1}{2} \times 10$-in. (19×25-cm) frame back

b. Press the picture onto the cardboard rectangle.

c. Use the scissors to trim away any parts of the picture that hang over the edge of the cardboard.

d. Repeat steps **2a**, **b**, and **c** to glue the second picture onto the other side of the cardboard.

e. Cut the puzzle into four differently shaped pieces, as shown.

f. Cut each of these pieces into two or more different pieces, so that you have between eight and 12 pieces. There is a suggested pattern on the next page.

3. Your Puzzle is ready to challenge you and your friends. Use the frame to store your puzzle and to keep the pieces in place while you try to solve the puzzle.

✪ **Even Better:** If the Puzzle is too easy, cut each piece into two pieces again.

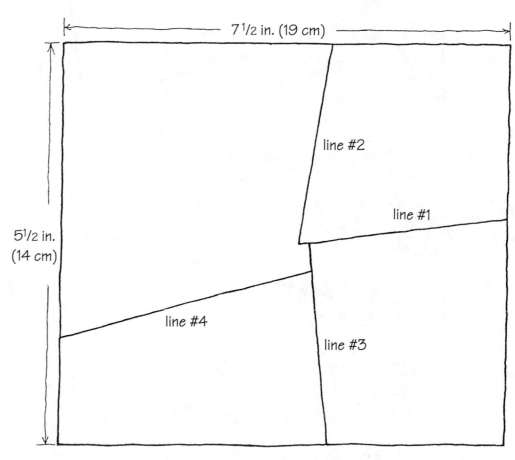

Cut the lines in the order that they are numbered.

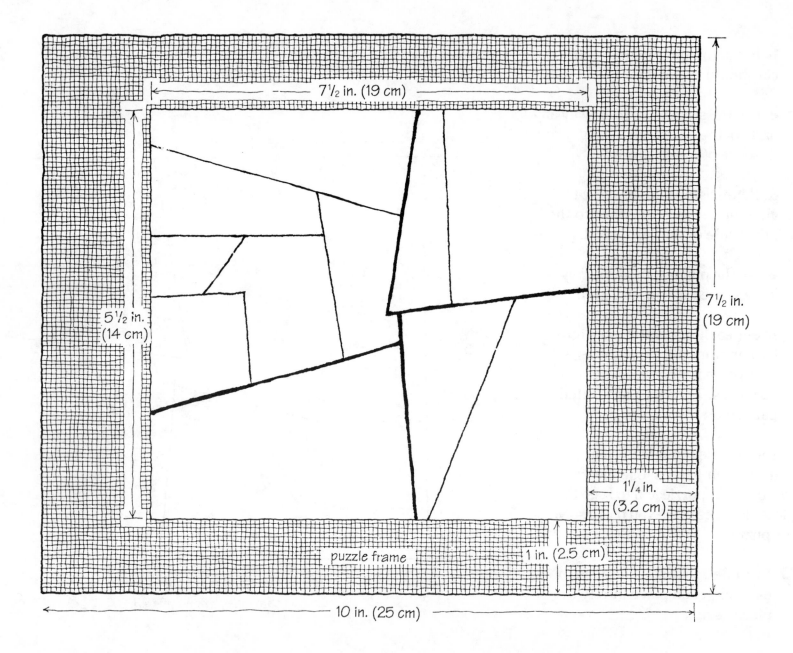

7½ in. (19 cm)

7½ in. (19 cm)

5½ in. (14 cm)

1¼ in. (3.2 cm)

puzzle frame

1 in. (2.5 cm)

10 in. (25 cm)

Ring-Toss

*This is a great game for a rainy day, and
a creative way to reuse an old box
and a bread-crumb carton.*

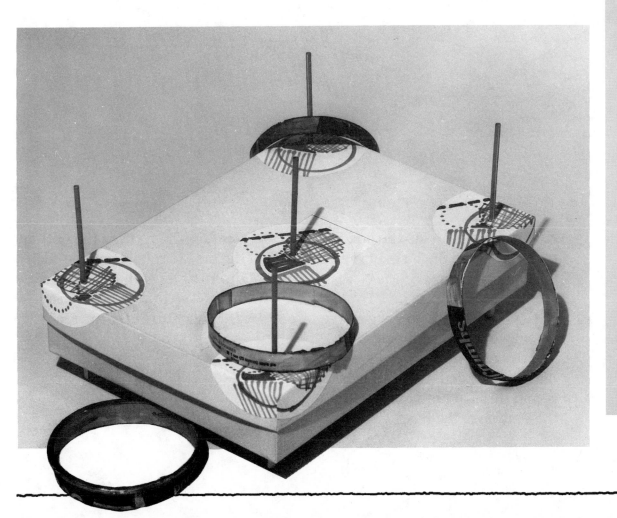

You Need

- [ ] a cardboard box with a removable lid about 8 × 6 × 2 inches (20 × 15 × 5 cm)
- [ ] five plastic coffee stirrers
- [ ] one cardboard cylinder-shaped carton about $3\frac{1}{4}$ inches (8.3 cm) in diameter (such as a bread-crumb carton)

Have on Hand

- [ ] $\frac{3}{4}$-inch (2-cm) masking tape

Tools

- [ ] a pencil
- [ ] a pushpin
- [ ] a ruler
- [ ] scissors

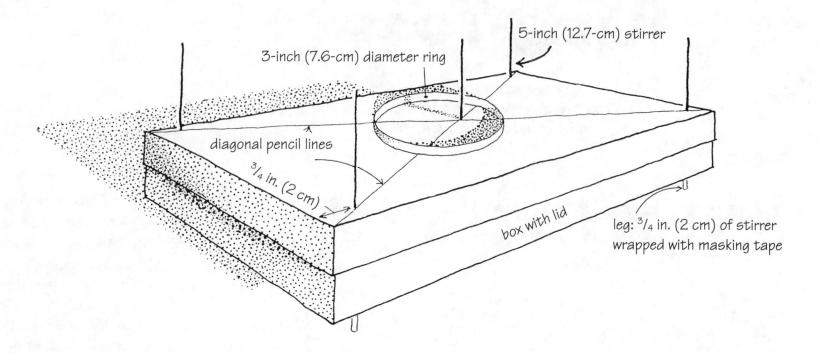

5-inch (12.7-cm) stirrer

3-inch (7.6-cm) diameter ring

diagonal pencil lines

³/₄ in. (2 cm)

box with lid

leg: ³/₄ in. (2 cm) of stirrer
wrapped with masking tape

Instructions

1. To make the game board:

a. Use the ruler and the pencil to draw light diagonal lines on the lid of the box. The lines cross at the center of the box.

b. Measure and mark points in each corner that are ³/₄ inch (2 cm) in from the short side.

c. Remove the lid, flip the box over, and place the lid over the bottom of the box.

d. Use the pushpin to poke a hole through each of the four marks and through the center, where the diagonal lines cross. Be sure to punch through both the lid and the bottom of the box.

e. Remove the lid from the bottom of the box. Carefully enlarge each of the 10 holes with the point of the pencil so that they are just large enough to fit the stirrers.

2. Wrap one end of each stirrer several times to make a thick blob of tape.

3. Place the stirrers up through the bottom of the box so that the masking tape is against the bottom.

   a. Align the stirrers in the holes on the lid. Carefully replace the lid onto the top of the box so that the stirrers come up through all the holes.

   b. Push the stirrers up through the box until the tape wrapped around them presses against the bottom of the box. These are the legs.

4. To make the rings:

   a. Use the ruler and the pencil to mark seven points up the cylindrical carton that are ¹/₂ inch (1.3 cm) apart.

   b. Repeat on the opposite side of the carton (be sure to measure from the same end). Connect the points by drawing rings around the carton.

   c. Use the Pushpin Method (see page 14) and scissors to cut out the rings.

5. To play:

   a. Set the game board on the floor.

   b. Place a pencil on the floor, at least 4 feet (1.2 m) away from the board, as a marker.

   c. Stand at the marker and throw the rings onto the stirrers.

   d. You score 5 points for the first ring you get on a stirrer. Two rings on the same stirrer is 15, and three is 30.

   e. Each player picks up the rings after his or her turn and hands them to the next player.

✪ **Even Better:** You can paint your game board and rings any way you want.

Recycling Facts & Tips

Did you know that:

- Each of us produces about 3¹/2 pounds (1.3 kg) of garbage each day.
- Nearly 80% of all the garbage we create is buried in landfills.

How you can help:

- You **can** make a difference! The best way to stand up against the tide of trash is to **educate** and **organize**. You can spread the word at home, at school, with your friends and neighbors, or anywhere you see other people. Together you and other people concerned with recycling can learn more and start a program to recycle trash that is currently being thrown away. See page 127 for more resources and ideas about how to start.

Cap & Can Game

This game is a great way to show your friends that you "can" recycle. We've used soup and tomato paste cans, but you can use any kind of cans you want.

You Need

- ☐ four clean, empty 16-ounce (472 ml) soup cans
- ☐ four clean, empty 6-ounce (177 ml) tomato paste cans

! **Note:** Have an **adult helper** make sure there are no sharp edges left around the open ends of the cans.

- ☐ four rubber bands

Have on Hand

- ☐ one friend
- ☐ a pencil
- ☐ six bottle caps

Instructions

1. All the cans should be clean and all the labels removed.

2. Put two rubber bands around two large soup cans to hold them together.

3. Pull out a part of the rubber bands and add the third large can.

4. Pull out a part of the rubber bands on the opposite side of the third can and add the fourth can.

5. Arrange the cans so that there is an even space in the middle, as shown.

6. Pull out the top rubber band so that you can fit a small can in the corner of two large cans, as shown. Now pull out the second rubber band and push the smaller can under it.

7. Use the same method to add the three other small cans, as shown.

8. Add one or two more rubber bands.

9. How to play:

   a. Place the cans on the floor.

   b. Place a pencil on the floor 6 feet (1.8 m) away from the cans.

   c. Stand behind the pencil and try to throw the bottle caps into the cans.

   d. You score 5 points for each cap that lands in a large can, 20 points for the small cans, and 30 for the space in the middle.

   e. Each player picks up the caps after his or her turn and hands the caps to the next player.

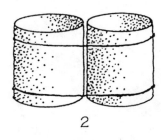

2

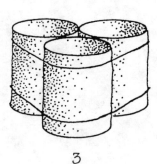

3

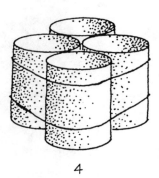

4

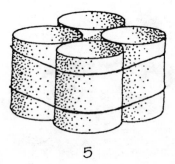

5

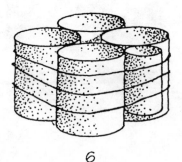

6

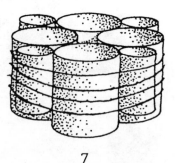

7

3-D Tic-Tac-Toe

This is just like regular Tic-Tac-Toe—you and your opponent are each trying to make a line of three Xs or three Os. But in 3-D Tic-Tac-Toe your line can be horizontal, vertical, or even diagonal.

Instructions

1. Use the pencil and the ruler to make a mark every 2 inches (5 cm) along each edge of the plain sides of the cardboard squares.

2. Draw lines connecting opposite marks to make a grid of 2-inch (5-cm) squares.

3. Cover your work area with newspaper.

4. Paint the grid in a checkerboard pattern with red and blue paint. (Alternate colors so that no two neighboring squares are the same.) Wait at least 20 minutes for the paint to dry before continuing.

5. Coat the unpainted sides of the squares with glue to prevent warping. Wait at least 20 minutes for the glue to dry.

6. Glue both ends of the cookie boxes shut. Wait at least 20 minutes for the glue to dry before going on to the next step.

7. Each of the cookie boxes has three slots to hold the game board. Mark and cut the slots as follows:

    a. One slot should be exactly in the middle of one edge of the boxes, as shown. You can measure 4 inches (10 cm) from either end.

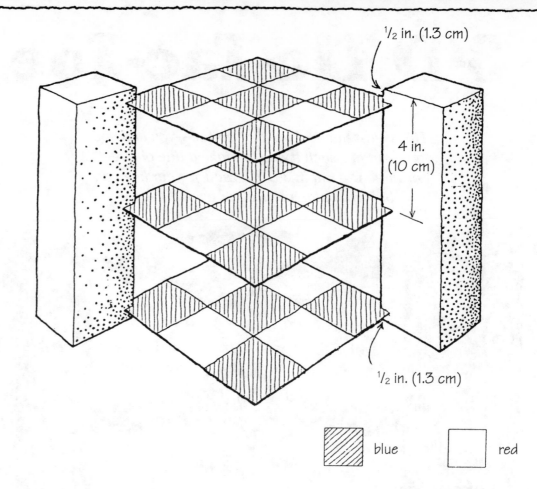

½ in. (1.3 cm)

4 in. (10 cm)

½ in. (1.3 cm)

blue   red

    b. The other two slots should each be ½ inch (1.3 cm) from the ends of the boxes, as shown.

    c. Use the Pushpin Method (see page 14) and scissors to cut these slots. The slots should extend ½ inch (1.3 cm) from either side of the corner.

8. Place the boards into the slots, as shown. You may need to adjust the slots to fit the boards tightly.

9. You're ready to play. Use one kind of bottle cap for **Xs** and the other kind for **Os**. Remember, your goal is to have your **Xs** or **Os** in three squares in a straight line. The trick is that the line can be horizontal, vertical, or diagonal.

Staying Earth-Friendly

In this book there are facts and tips about trash, recycling, and how you can help save the Earth.

If you want more information about how you can help, you can write to the groups listed here. These organizations can give you ideas and information about reducing, reusing, and recyling.

Don't forget about your local resources. Parents, teachers, neighbors and friends probably have lots of information about how your community recycles.

Organizations

Coalition for a Recyclable Waste Stream
1525 New Hampshire Ave., NW
Washington, DC 20036
(301) 891-1100

The Environmental Action Coalition
625 Broadway
Second Floor
New York, NY 10012
(212) 677-1601

Environmental Defense Fund
475 Park Ave. South
New York, NY 10016
(800) CALL-EDF

Inform
381 Park Ave. South
New York, NY 10016
(212) 689-4040

Keep America Beautiful
Mill River Plaza
9 West Broad St.
Stamford, CT 06902
(203) 323-8987

National Recycling Coalition
1101 30th St., NW
Washington, DC 20007
(202) 625-6406

Natural Resource Defense Council
40 West 20th St.
New York, NY 10011
(212) 727-2700

Other Books

If you've enjoyed reading *Earth-Friendly Toys*, you might also enjoy these books:

About Garbage and Stuff.
Ann A. Shanks, Viking Press,
New York, 1973.

Cartons, Cans, and Orange Peels:
Where Does Your Garbage Go?
Joanna Foster, Clarion Books,
New York, 1991.

Earth Book for Kids: Activities to
Help Heal the Environment.
Linda Schwartz, The Learning Works,
Santa Barbara, Calif., 1990.

The Kid's Guide to Social Action.
Barbara A. Lewis, Free Spirit
Publishing, Minneapolis, 1991.

The Lorax. Dr. Seuss,
Random House, New York, 1988.

Taking Out the Trash:
A No-Nonsense Guide to Recycling.
Jennifer Carfess, Island Press,
Washington, D.C., 1992.